"The dignity of the person is the bedrock of any society with a human face. But if the last century witnessed some of history's greatest violations, the coming century may well prove worse. *A Time for Dignity* is an urgent call for Christians. If ever the biblical view of individuals made in the image of God was important, it is today as the age of biogenetic engineering accelerates and the promise of trans-humanism approaches. Followers of Jesus must not fail to rise to the challenge of the hour."

—Os Guinness, author and social critic

# A Time for Dignity

Crisis and Gospel Today

Other Books by Mel Lawrenz

*Spiritual Influence: the Hidden Power Behind Leadership*

*Life After Grief*

*I Want to Believe*

*How to Understand the Bible: A Simple Guide*

*Knowing Him*

*Overcoming Guilt and Shame*

*Whole Church: From Fragmentation to Engagement*

# A Time for Dignity
## Crisis and Gospel Today

Mel Lawrenz

WWW.WORDWAY.ORG

# Group Discussion

Use *A Time for Dignity* in a group discussion of anywhere from one to five sessions. Consider using these questions for each discussion:

• I learned these important things from the reading. . .

• The reading made me wonder about. . .

• I am confused, troubled, or disturbed about. . .

• I believe these points in the reading apply to my life or my work at this time. . . .

Consider also sharing your thoughts online at:
www.wordway.org/dignity

# CONTENTS

# Introduction

Four years ago the issue of human dignity and the gospel came to my attention when I was with Christian leaders in India, who described their mission as the restoration of the dignity of people discarded by most of society. Then I met leaders in Latin America and Africa and North America using the same description. I started doing some research and quickly concluded that "dignity" is an ideal widely held, but not deeply understood.

This book is intended to prompt reflection and discussion about dignity not just as a philosophical concept, but as an everyday reality. We live in times when we have complex ethical decisions that depend on our understanding of human worth; when our public life in our media, entertainment, and politics frequently is coarse and dehumanizing; and when Christians have unlimited opportunities to help people beaten down by life's circumstances.

Chapter 1 describes the struggle for dignity and the meaning of dignity, including its connection with the gospel of Christ. Chapter 2 looks at the dark backdrop of corruption in the human family, and some of the main ways we experience indignity and diminishment. Then in chapter 3 we look at the promise of the restoration of dignity, which leads to chapter 4 on dignity and the mandate of the Christian gospel. This mandate includes eight main areas where our commitments are critical today. Finally, in chapter 5 we consider the dignity of Jesus—both in his person as the perfect image of the perfect God, and in his suffering the worst kinds of indignity possible.

I hope this book will help in several ways. First, that these reflections on dignity and the gospel will offer hope to people who have experienced personal diminishment in some way. Second, to prompt us to action as defenders of dignity in the name of Christ. Third, to affirm those who are already laboring to work against the dehumanizing dynamics that keep people in crisis and bondage.

There is a danger in offering a relatively short book on such a wide-ranging topic, but I wanted to show the connectedness of a great range of issues, knowing that this is just the start of deeper reflections.

Dignity is an issue of monumental importance. There are those today who say perhaps we should give up on the longing for dignity, and those who say dignity is nothing more than personal autonomy. We are being invited to give up our souls. This must not happen.

I could not have written this book without one familiar and unwelcome companion: hardship. It would be easy to write about dignity in a superficially idealistic way. But we do not need one more cliché, and certainly not a glib characterization of the gospel. We can only understand dignity against the backdrop of suffering and depravity.

Believing in dignity is only possible when we look honestly at the many faces of indignity, admit where we have been responsible for diminishing others, and face where we ourselves have been diminished. So, in a way, I am glad that in the years I've been studying the topic of dignity, I've seen its necessity through family hardships, illness, and professional disappointments. And I am humbled to know so many people in so many parts of the world who have had to endure pain and insecurity and dismay, but still hold on to the truth that what God values no one can destroy.

*Chapter 1*

---

# What Is a Human Being Worth?

---

*So many roads, so much at stake*
*So many dead ends, I'm at the edge of the lake*
*Sometimes I wonder what it's gonna take*
*To find dignity.*
*—Bob Dylan, "Dignity"*

Some years back a friend of mine in Addis Ababa, Ethiopia, took me to see the largest hospital in Africa for people with leprosy. I was wondering why I was feeling a little apprehensive about going, and then I realized it was because of the powerful biblical allusions to people afflicted with leprosy and the dreadful treatment they received as outcasts of society. Though leprosy (today known as Hansen's disease) is now treatable, there are still thousands of cases a year that develop in impoverished parts of the world. Up until the end of the 20th century, there were still leper colonies where these poor souls were consigned to lives of hopelessness and isolation, dehumanized by disease, and shunned by their fellow man.

We walked through this hospital and rehabilitation center where men and women sat on benches or on the floor, some of them doing handiwork, others unable to do so because their fingers were missing or their hands were deformed into claw-like appendages. The disease can also have a degenerative effect on the face, destroying noses, turning the skin into deep, lumpy wrinkles.

Any serious disease threatens to diminish our humanity—our dignity. This hospital, founded in 1928 by medical missionary Dr. Thomas Lambie, existed to help people not become the debris of the human race, to hold on to a kind of dignity that not even leprosy can take away.

This, of course, is exactly what Jesus did in his encounters with people afflicted with leprosy. He touched them—a taboo. He had supper at the table of Simon the Leper. He told his disciples to reach out with healing power to people with leprosy, and with that, to proclaim the gospel: "the kingdom of heaven has come near" (Matt. 10:7-8).

## The Struggle for Dignity

Despite all the painful circumstances of life that can make us feel incomplete, or less than fully human, most people do not give up the hope that they have some worth, some dignity. Illness makes us less than whole. Aging diminishes the body and oftentimes the mind. Abusive relationships violate. Loss and trauma fracture people's lives like earthquakes that weaken the whole structure of life. Unemployment and under-employment rob people of a sense of purpose. Many who have a job work for managers who treat them like gears in a machine.

Yet most people hope there is something higher about personhood that cannot be taken away. Most people want to hold their heads up.

We also struggle to find dignity because of the coarseness and profanity and rudeness we have learned to accept as cultural norms. Dignity is about respect, including self-respect; yet it is now common to reward those whose voices are the most disrespectful, vulgar, tasteless, insolent, insulting, disparaging, and obscene. Our eyes are glazed over by the television screen and the smartphone as we wait for someone who jolts us enough so that we know are still alive. Celebrity can still mean fame for notable accomplishments; but in a media-drenched world, celebrity can be an achievement unto itself, the ability to be famous merely by getting noticed—no matter what it takes.

In this kind of culture, it almost sounds silly to talk about dignified behavior. But it may also be what people most crave.

As if the natural struggles of life were not enough, we live in a time when people are deciding philosophically whether to hold on to dignity or give it up. Cynics are saying we never should have imagined in the first place that human beings are anything other than relatively advanced animals. Atheists are asserting that dignity is a concept that has always had spiritual or religious overtones and should be discarded like the toddler clothing we left behind when we grew out of childhood. Killers who believe in jihad use techniques designed not just to kill, but to take away all dignity.

There is also great confusion over the meaning of dignity. Those who still hold the ideal of dignity have entirely different ideas of its meaning. Legal experts, for instance, are torn on what dignity means and whether it should even figure into major judgments. In opinions of the Supreme Court of the United States, the term *dignity* appears nearly a thousand times, but "despite its popularity, dignity is a concept in disarray. Its meanings and functions are commonly presupposed but rarely articulated. The result is a cacophony of uses so confusing that some critics argue the word ought to be abandoned altogether." [1]

## What Is Dignity?

This much we know: the word "dignity" is rooted in the Latin *dignitas*, from *dignus*, "worthy." [2] Dignity is about worth. Does a man or woman, boy or girl, have real worth? A foundation upon which to build a worthwhile life? A reason to behave respectably? A right to be treated justly?

Dignity is one of those concepts we assume is commonly understood. But when we look more closely we find that different people's ideas of worth diverge into multiple, contradictory streams. Today, human dignity is the subject of a new array of books raising the question of whether we need to stop and look at what dignity actually means.[3]

One baseline understanding of dignity is worth as an inherent characteristic. Like the $20 bill in your wallet that has an objective and unalterable value—whether it's crisp and clean, or wrinkled and soiled—the value or worth is assigned by an external authority and thus cannot be denied or assailed. This is the historic biblical concept of human worth. Every human being, no matter how tattered and worn and sullied, has an inherent worth, determined by his or her Creator. This is why a fireman standing outside a burning building, hearing a scream inside, does not calculate what kind of human being is crying out for rescue before he plunges into the smoke. No matter their age or gender or race or any other variable in the human family, all human beings are worth saving because they possess the same essential worth.

A different view holds that dignity or worth has to do with social status.[4] In societies or communities with any rigid class system, if you are born into an upper level, you have worth. If you are born into the lower class, too bad for you. You have worth if you live in a certain part of town, have access to a higher quality of schools, have money in the bank. Worth comes from privilege.[5] This was the concept of dignity in classical times. In the Roman Empire, for instance, if you were born into the upper class, you possessed honor or dignity. If you were born into the slave class, you simply had no *dignitas*.

A third way of speaking about dignity is related to behavior. People who conduct themselves in a "dignified" manner have worth because they are living it. They show respect toward others, they behave with decorum, they have manners, they are principled and are known for their integrity. Even if they do not have social status, they have a compelling inner motivation to behave in a dignified way. This certainly is an attractive idea. Who wouldn't want more people in the world today to behave better? The question is whether dignity comes from behavior, or the other way around, that good behavior is a consequence of dignity.

A more recent view of dignity—and one with profound consequences—sees worth in one thing only: autonomy. Dignity is the right to do what you wish to do without interference from anyone else or the laws of the state. Dignity is self-determination. It may have no ethical or moral content. Dignity is not defined by any external authority.

Physician-assisted suicide, for instance, has for years been promoted under the catchphrase "death with dignity." That is an easy slogan but full of contradictions.

A microphone caught the words of a frantic preacher calling out to hundreds of followers on a fateful day in November of 1978. "Lay down your life with dignity. Don't lay down with tears and agony. There's nothing to death. We must die with some dignity. We must die with some dignity. We will have no choice. Now we have some choice."

In the minutes that followed in Jonestown, Guyana, more than 900 people drank the cyanide-laced drink prepared by Reverend Jim Jones. It was the largest mass suicide in history.

In 2003, bioethicist Ruth Macklin, in an article in the *BMJ* (*British Medical Journal*) entitled "Dignity Is a Useless Concept," argued that appeals to human dignity in the field of medical ethics "are either vague restatements of other, more precise, notions or mere slogans that add nothing to an understanding of the topic." We would do well to give up the idea, she argues, unless we limit it to autonomy, which protects all that really matters: our "life, body, and freedom."

Several years later Harvard psychologist Steven Pinker echoed Macklin's concern in an essay in *The New Republic* (May 2008) entitled "The Stupidity of Dignity." Pinker, like Macklin, wanted to shut down any dignity-oriented ethical discussions of human cloning, genetic engineering, stem cell research, and other newer forms of research and treatment. "The problem is that 'dignity' is a squishy, subjective notion, hardly up to the heavyweight moral demands assigned to it," according to Pinker. Informed consent is all that is needed for bioethical decisions, anything else is an imposition of the values of others. "Dignity is a useless concept" because it necessarily imposes the ethical standards of one group on another.

Dignity is one of those ideals that comes up everywhere in public discourse, but it gets contradicted all the time. People don't know whether dignity is a treasure, a cost, or both.

## Dignity as Inherent Worth

If it is true that all people have inherent or intrinsic worth, this will be rooted in origins. Otherwise it would not be intrinsic (i.e., innate, inborn, natural, integral, essential).[6] That is why we view the story of creation in the book of

Genesis as a historic definition of human worth. Genesis describes the essential characteristics of humanity from the beginning. Genesis 1:26-27 is that description:

> Then God said, "Let us make mankind in our image, in our likeness, so that they may rule over the fish in the sea and the birds in the sky, over the livestock and all the wild animals, and over all the creatures that move along the ground." So God created mankind in his own image, in the image of God he created them; male and female he created them.

"In our image, in our likeness"—this nexus of divine and human is the essential idea of humanity at the beginning of the Hebrew Scriptures, an idea carried forward into the New Testament. The meaning is expansive and somewhat elusive. What could this mean, that man and woman are created according to the image and likeness of God?

The Hebrew words for "image" (*selem*) and "likeness" (*demut*) are synonymous in this passage, pointing to the ideal that human beings are designed to be like God. This does not mean human beings are little deities (later uses of *image* in the Old Testament point to the deceptiveness of manmade idols), but beings created with the ideal of being like God in some ways. But in what ways? The passage does not explicitly explain what this means, which has led to various theories.

Some have said that *creativity* is a human trait that mirrors the creative nature of God, though no man or woman has ever created something out of nothing. No one supposes himself or herself capable of declaring anything like, "Let there be light." Human beings may be creative, but they are not the Creator. Any person could sit down today with drawing paper and a pencil, and sketch the floor plan of a house that no one has ever conceived before. The birds that return to your backyard, on the other hand, always build their nests in exactly the same pattern, determined solely by animal instinct. We find no apartment complexes in the trees.

*Spirituality* is another capability of humanity that relates to God. God is spirit; people are spiritual beings. All people are spiritual beings, whether they are conscious of their spirituality or not. Any time we whisper a prayer, or have a sense of the numinous while sitting in a church sanctuary, or experience a moment of comfort when-hearing Psalm 23 read at a funeral, we are showing our innate spirituality.

Then there is *intelligence*. God is a rational being, and human beings are capable of rational thought, analysis, and expression. That is not to say that we comprehend everything. The highest form of truth exceeds our capacity to comprehend, because our limited and fallible minds do not fathom all reality. Yet there is a world of truth we can understand and discuss and propagate. Otherwise, we'd have no spiritual discussions. We would stare blankly when we we'd exhausted all conversations about what we ate today, how hard it's raining outside, and whether our favorite TV show is doing a rerun. We can do more than that. We *must* do more than that or else we have no hope of addressing any of our personal problems, national ills, and global crises.

Others have pointed out that our sense of *morality* must be derived from the nature of a Creator God who is an essentially moral being. Human beings have a sense of right and wrong; ought and ought not; good, better, and best. Even very young children cry out at the injustice of getting their toys stolen by other children. Moral indignation. Righteous anger. Forensic analysis. "That's not *fair!*"

Now that hasn't stopped many people from rejecting the notion that there are moral standards that they have to be subject to. That is, until their next door neighbor plants a tree on the wrong side of the lot line or lets his dog relieve himself in the wrong yard. Then the "ought/ought not" principle comes to the fore—with a vengeance. And if we think we can separate matters of law and civic regulation from morality, we should note there is no law that is not, in essence, some extension of moral imperative. Morality does not take something from us; it is at the core of our worth.

Finally, many biblical interpreters have noted that in the Genesis passage the language may link *community* or *relationship* with the concept of being created in the image and likeness of God. "Let *us* make humanity in *our* image, in *our* likeness" (italics added). A classic Christian interpretation is that this is the triune God at work in creation: Father, Son, and Holy Spirit determining to do this wondrous thing, to make a category of creatures who are Godlike. This is why we have the capacity and the need to exist in community. We are like God in that spouses and relatives and friends and coworkers can relish the benefits of each other's companionship.

Dr. John Kilner, in his major work on dignity and the image of *God, Dignity and Destiny: Humanity in the Image of God* (Eerdmans, 2015), offers a significant adjustment to these traditional views. Kilner shows how the Genesis passage describes humanity as created *according to* the image of God, but that it really is only Jesus Christ who *is* the image of God. The development of sin in the human race causes people to become broken; it is not the image of God which is broken. That remains intact as that ideal that is the destiny of humanity. Kilner warns that if we think the image is damaged in sin, then that is an opening for the oft-repeated cycles of abuse and oppression we see in history.

Made according to the image and likeness of God. Though not explained explicitly in Genesis, it is fair to think this means human beings have a grace-based dignity and destiny.

And this is why a human being is worth something.

## What Is a Person Worth?

Ninety-nine percent of a human body consists of six elements: oxygen, carbon, hydrogen, nitrogen, calcium, and phosphorus. The remaining one percent consists of minor elements and trace elements. If you purchased these chemicals on the market, you would have to spend a bit more than $100.

Most of us believe people are worth more than $100.

Yet not everyone. The Nazis considered Jews, homosexuals, Poles, mentally ill people, and others to be of no worth whatsoever. Of negative worth, in fact, worthy only of extermination since they were viewed as a net deficit in the human race.

I went to see Auschwitz in the south of Poland one summer day. Seeing the place in films and still photos is one thing; walking into its netherworld-like reality is another. There it all is: the underground bunker disguised as a giant group shower with holes in the ceiling where the Zyklon B was dropped in; the pallets on mechanized tracks that delivered bodies to the gaping holes of the ovens; the endless rows of barracks built alongside railroad tracks for the efficient herding of victims. Somehow what hit me as hard as the piles of eyeglasses and suitcases and hair, were the mechanisms of this death factory. Carts and tracks and ovens—and rusting spare parts on the side. Human beings did this. They built a machinery of mass desecration and with it millions perished.

The evil irony of it all is that the perpetrators were acting out of a perverse sense of superiority, a kind of exaggerated, twisted dignity. Such monsters were able to treat human beings as refuse only because they saw themselves as gods. The ultimate form of idolatry is viewing the self as sovereign. And it is not only Nazis who view life that way.

These realities of history show us how radically wrong we can get the dignity equation. The jagged road of history twists this way and that between defaming people and deifying them. This is exactly why we need to get the dignity equation right.

## Is Dignity a Biblical Concept?

It is fair to ask whether dignity is a biblical concept. English translations of the Bible typically have only a handful of verses in which the word is used. Of course important words like *Trinity* or *omnipotent*, *omnipresent*, *omniscient* never appear in Scripture itself. The word *attribute* does not appear in Scripture, nor *theology*. The word *Bible* never appears in the Bible.

The question needs to be whether the *idea* of dignity is in Scripture. If we take the word in its simplest sense—worth or worthiness—it certainly is. The creation of humankind is all about value or worth, God-given. The whole sweep of redemption history through the Old and New Testaments presumes that God did many things for the restoration of humanity, not because God had to, but because God considered it worthwhile to do so. In the sacrifice of Jesus we see the highest value. "God so loved the world that he gave his only Son," not because humanity was worthy, but because God considered it worthwhile to do.

Dignity is a quality of humanity because of two great divine acts: creation and redemption. Worth creating; worth saving. None of us would risk our lives to snatch a photo album from a burning house, but we would put our lives on the line to save a human being. And the rescued person, if he or she is thinking right, will take that moment of rescue as a radical redirection of his or her life because he or she can see that someone else has proclaimed their value.

## Dignity and Gospel

My own thinking about dignity and the gospel began when I was teaching in India. I was working with an organization seeking to raise the real-life conditions of the Dalits, the so-called "untouchables." I visited the schools and the clinics and the vocational training centers where people who were considered worthless in society were shown a little dignity, and even a way to find dignity. School kids with clean uniforms, sitting in rows before the blackboard and a qualified teacher, for instance.

I was taken to one of the schools in a rural area where, as our car drove up the dusty road, several hundred children had just lined up in rows in an outer courtyard to honor us with singing and recitations. The sun beat down hot on the dusty courtyard, but the children beamed with smiles, wearing their white and blue school uniforms and shouting their memorizations. To be admitted to the school, to leave tattered clothes for bright uniforms, to have the opportunity to learn to read and write, is to attain a sense of personal worth—of true dignity.

One day there was a discussion about a mission statement for this effort. We talked about how it was important not to conceive of the mission as *giving* dignity to these suffering and persecuted people. If we can give dignity to someone, we can also take it away. No, it must be phrased as "recognizing" or "affirming" or "defending" or "restoring" dignity.

I noticed other Christian workers in other countries describing their work in terms of helping people restore their dignity. This is not separate from proclaiming the gospel, the good news of salvation in Jesus Christ. It is the expression of it. If God's great saving act is to restore human Godlikeness, then dignity is part and parcel of the gospel.

In one of his latter books, John Stott put it this way:

Christian teaching on the dignity and worth of human beings is of the utmost importance today, not only for the sake of our own self-image and self-respect, but even more for the welfare of society. When human beings are devalued, everything in society turns sour. Women are humiliated and children despised. The sick are regarded as a nuisance, and the elderly as a burden. Ethnic minorities as discriminated against. The poor are oppressed and denied social justice. . . . Labour is exploited in the mines and factories. Criminals are brutalized in prison. . . . There is no freedom, no dignity, no carefree joy. Human life seems not worth living, because it is scarcely human any longer. But when human beings are valued as persons, because of their intrinsic worth, everything changes. Men, women and children are all honoured. The sick are cared for, and the elderly enabled to live and die with dignity. Dissidents are listened to, prisoners rehabilitated, minorities protected, and the oppressed set free. Workers are given fair wages, decent working conditions, and a measure of participation in both the management and the profit of the enterprise. And the gospel is taken to the ends of the earth. Why? Because people matter. Because every man, woman and child has worth and significance as a human being made in God's image and likeness. [7]

*This is a time for dignity.*

But to work toward the restoration of dignity for our neighbors and friends nearby and around the world, we will have to work through complicated issues. For instance:

- What if one person's view of dignity calls into question another person's actions? If dignity is a value judgment, does that make it an imposition?
- Do acts of evil and malice contradict the principle of dignity?
- Can a person lose his or her value?
- What is the relationship between freedom and dignity?
- Are human beings both dignified and depraved?
- What is a credible response to the idea that dignity is an invalid or outdated concept?
- Is dignity a universal and cross-cultural ideal, or is it only a Western concept?
- What distinguishes a Christian view of dignity from secular versions of the concept? What are we to make of the arguments for human rights based in historic statements like the Universal Declaration of Human Rights (1948)?
- Can people suffering extreme abuse or enslavement really gain a sense of personal dignity?
- What are the front line issues today which the gospel must be applied to?

It is one thing to insist on one's own worth and rights; it is another to stand up for the worth of others. Dignity is not merely a concept; it must be a cause. If this is a time for dignity, it is not for the purpose of trying very hard to feel better about ourselves. It does not begin with attempts at solving personal or societal problems. It is a matter of becoming human again.

---

[1] Leslie Meltzer Henry, "The Jurisprudence of Dignity," *University of Pennsylvania Law Review* 160 (2011): 169.

[2] Our English *dignity* has a wide semantic range. Most English dictionaries list the primary meaning of *dignity* as worth or the quality of being worthy (of respect, honor, etc.) with related meanings regarding behavior, attitude, or social status. The Latin *dignitas* in the ancient Roman world referred more narrowly to social status.

3 Some of the newer books exploring the theme of dignity include: Michael Rosen, *Dignity: Its History and Meaning* (Cambridge: Harvard University Press, 2012); David Gushee, *The Sacredness of Human Life: Why an Ancient Biblical Vision Is Key to the World's Future* (Grand Rapids, Eerdmans, 2013); John Kilner, *Dignity and Destiny: Humanity in the Image of God*, (Grand Rapids: Eerdmans, 2015); Marcus Düwell et al., ed. *The Cambridge Handbook of Human Dignity: Interdisciplinary Perspectives* (Cambridge: Cambridge University Press, 2014); George Kateb, *Human Dignity* (Cambridge: Belknap Press, 2011). Donna Hicks, *Dignity: Its Essential Role in Resolving Conflict* (New Haven: Yale University Press, 2013); Leon Kass, *Life, Liberty and the Defense of Dignity* (San Francisco: Encounter Books, 2002); and Robert Kraynak, Glenn Tinder, ed., *In Defense of Human Dignity: Essays for Our Times* (Notre Dame, Indiana: University of Notre Dame Press, 2003).

4 "'Dignity' [in Latin] originated as a concept that denoted high social status and the honors and respectful treatment that are due to someone who occupied that position." Rosen, *Dignity: Its History and Meaning*, 11.

5 Even if the classical idea of dignity is fundamentally tied into rank, it is possible to move toward a more egalitarian ideal, according to Jeremy Waldron: "Dignity, we are told, was once tied up with rank: the dignity of a king was not the same as the dignity of bishop and neither of them was the same as the dignity of a professor. If our modern conception of human dignity retains any scintilla of its ancient and historical connection with rank— and I think it does: I think it expresses the idea of the high and equal rank of every human person." Jeremy Waldron, *Dignity, Rank, and Rights* (Oxford: Oxford University Press, 2012), 14.

[6] David Gushee, in his substantial *The Sacredness of Human Life*, says that the biblical vision of dignity is that it is God-given, not "inherent." But many others use the word *inherent* with the idea that the trait is innate because it is God-given.

[7] John Stott, *The Contemporary Christian* (Downers Grove: IVP Books, 1995), 232.

*Chapter 2*

## Slap in the Face:
## The Insult of Indignity

*Any man or institution that tries to rob
me of my dignity will lose.*

—*Nelson Mandela*

Shark attacks, torturous thirst, body-numbing hunger, terrifying nighttime storms, Japanese strafing runs. These were some of the hardships that reduced Louis Zamperini and his two fellow soldiers to hollow men drifting for weeks in tattered rubber rafts on the vast Pacific Ocean after their crippled plane ditched in the sea. Laura Hillenbrand describes the story in her best-selling book, *Unbroken*. Telling the part of the story when the men became

POWs in a succession of Japanese prison camps, she writes:

> The crash of *Green Hornet* had left Louie and Phil in the most desperate physical extremity, without food, water, or shelter. But on Kwajalein [a prison camp island], the guards sought to deprive them of something that had sustained them even as all else had been lost: dignity. This self-respect and sense of self-worth, the innermost armament of the soul, lies at the heart of humanness; to be deprived of it is to be dehumanized, to be cleaved from, and cast below, mankind. Men subjected to dehumanizing treatment experience profound wretchedness and loneliness and find that hope is almost impossible to retain. Without dignity, identity is erased. In its absence, men are defined not by themselves, but by their captors and the circumstances in which they are forced to live. One American airman, shot down and relentlessly debased by his Japanese captors, described the state of mind that his captivity created: "I was literally becoming a lesser human being."

Few societies treasured dignity and feared humiliation as did the Japanese, for whom a loss of honor could merit suicide. This is likely one of the reasons why Japanese soldiers during World War II debased their prisoners with such zeal, seeking to take from them that which was most painful and destructive to lose. On Kwajalein, Louie and Phil learned a dark truth known to the doomed in Hitler's death camps, the slaves of the America South, and a hundred other generations of betrayed people. Dignity is as essential to human life as water, food, and oxygen. The stubborn retention of it, even in the face of extreme physical hardship, can hold a man's soul in his body long past the point at which the body should have surrendered it. The loss of it can carry a man off as surely as thirst, hunger, exposure, and asphyxiation, and with greater cruelty. In places like Kwajalein, degradation could be as lethal as a bullet. [1]

In an interview in the *The New York Times* in February 2003, Louis Zamperini himself said: "I could take the beatings and the physical punishment, but it was-the attempt to destroy your dignity, to make you a nonentity, that was the hardest thing to bear."

## The Insult of Indignity

We know that dignity is important because of belief in the intent of the Creator as expressed in Scripture, and because we have so many examples of people aspiring to hold on to their dignity. But another reason we know it is important is that when we experience indignity, the wounding and the insult cut so deep.

This is everyday experience, not just the extreme examples of prisoners of war and Holocaust victims. Indignity is the experience of the woman ridiculed behind her back by coworkers because of her physical appearance, the man who is impotent following prostate cancer, the teenage girl who is bullied at school, the boy who is battling leukemia. It is the elderly couple whose opinion is not taken seriously anymore simply because they have more history than future. It is Christians in the Middle East leaving their native countries in vast numbers in the face of death threats. It is refugees pouring out of Syria with no idea where they can lay their heads.

Everyday indignity is the woman who keeps remembering sexual abuse from decades earlier, which has shaped her life. Racism—that belief that one race is superior to another—is the rejection of worth of a whole class of people. The insult of indignity is seen in every instance of gossip, malicious rumor, and intentional public demeaning. There is no limit to the number of ways people try to reduce other people.

## Dignity or Depravity or Both?

It will come as no surprise that some people believe dignity is a false hope because what they see in the human race, in their communities, or in their families is deplorable and vile. Like the photojournalist who makes a decision where to point the camera, some of us tend to focus on people and events that are honorable, and other people focus on what is odious. The camera sees both because both are true of humanity. Dignity is real, but so is depravity.

At the beginning of the 20th century, optimism was running high. The Industrial Revolution was in full swing, impacting every aspect of daily life. Income was on a steady rise and with it a better standard of living for most people. Scientists, engineers, and inventors were dazzling the world. The use of electricity was expanding. Henry Ford introduced the automobile. The Wright brothers achieved powered flight after a surge of innovation and years of toil. Hundreds of thousands of laborers were digging a channel between the Atlantic and Pacific in Panama. Radio changed the face of communication. Great ocean liners crisscrossed the globe. Artists and musicians were expressing themselves in bold new forms.

And Christianity was expanding. In the 100 years before 1900, the gospel of Christ had, for the first time, become a global proclamation with a modern missionary movement that would change the world. The 1910 World Missionary Conference in Edinburgh, Scotland, brought together 1,200 representatives—almost the whole spectrum of Protestant denominations, an unprecedented gathering. For some, there was little doubt that peace and prosperity, and even the kingdom of Christ expressed in social realities, had finally triumphed in the troubled human family.

But in 1914 everything changed. The long era of peace and prosperity, of hope and optimism, turned into a dark new era of the whole world at war. In a bitter historical irony, the very day the first steamship passed through the newly completed Panama Canal on August 3, 1914, Germany declared war on France and invaded Belgium. The Panama Canal was the greatest engineering feat in history, an accomplishment which promised to raise the prosperity of the whole world, achieved by a gargantuan effort over decades, with thousands of lives lost. But on the first day it was used, this unprecedented human achievement was eclipsed by the start of mankind's worst nightmare.

What we know as World War I was (naively) called at the time "the war to end all wars." But just two decades later, another world war erupted, one that would leave 55 million human beings dead. The inventiveness of humanity made possible mustard gas in the trenches during World War I, and ended with fission bombs over Hiroshima and Nagasaki to end World War II. Just five years after the end of World War II, war broke out on the Korean peninsula.

Troublesome indignities in the human family lead to war, and follow war, and are starkly evident in the destruction of human beings made in the image of God during war. The occasional necessity of war and even the-

camaraderie and heroism of soldiers do not erase the self-evident truth that war represents the moral failure of humanity and its worst form of indignity.

Peace is out of reach not because the hope for something noble in life is naive, but because it is unwanted. The harshest tragedy is when people give up their dignity simply because they do not want it. This presents us with a great mystery: why is it that we squander the best of what we are?

## Being Bent

In *Out of the Silent Planet*, the first in a trilogy of science fiction novels, C. S. Lewis's characters discuss corruption and evil in the human race with a simple image. Humanity is "bent," twisted by a malevolent spirit called "The Bent One." One character observes, "a bent hnau [i.e., human] can do more evil than a broken one."[2] It is true. Deception comes from something that seems to be good. Our worst enemies look like friends. The worst toxins to the human soul taste delicious.

Throughout Lewis's writings he repeats the Augustinian understanding of sin and evil as good things gone bad. "Bent." This is biblical, and it avoids the mistaken idea that evil is an existence itself. This is why dignity in this life may become corrupted, but not absolutely lost. "Bentness" is corruption, not destruction. And "bent ones" can be restored to their original form. In this is hope.

The Protestant Reformers of the 16th century described depravity as the idea that there is not one function or characteristic of human nature that is not twisted in some way. It is not that everything in the world is as bad as it can possibly be. It is not that people always make every mistake they can ever make. It does not mean that the image of God in humanity is destroyed. Depravity means we live with and must compensate for the reality that all our motives and actions and desires are distorted to some degree. Human nature is deformed. The ways in which we are created to be like God are the very ways we can practice evil. Creativity can serve evil ends. Intellect can perceive what is true, but it can also perpetuate false assumptions and construct monstrous philosophies. Morality vacillates. The conscience may be calloused or oversensitive. Spirituality sometimes chases false gods.

And so we live with this grinding incongruity: dignity with depravity.

Perhaps the greatest irony of the dignity/depravity tension is that something truly bad can only come from the corruption of something truly good. Think about it. Who is most able to hurt you—a stranger, or someone you love? Who is most able to disappoint you—someone you never respected, or someone you admired or even revered? Who does more damage—an atheist, or a believer who has become an atheist?

We would have no sense of depravity if we had no expectation of dignity in the first place. And so, with all of creation we groan under the stresses of a good world gone wrong. But unless we become despondent and hopeless, we keep longing for something better. It is not naive to do so.

## Indignity Through Abuse

Indignity has many faces, and one of the ugliest is abuse.

The second time the idea of humanity made in the image of God appears in Scripture is in Genesis 9. Following the narrative of the flood, there is a kind of reset for the human race, including this principle: "Whoever sheds human blood, by humans shall their blood be shed for in the image of God has God made mankind" (Gen. 9:6).

What is important here is the *reason* it is wrong for someone to injure or murder another: "for in the image of God has God made mankind." [3] When one person violates another, it is not just a slap to the face of another person; it is a slap to the face of God.

This is the specific reason why murder and abuse and racism are immoral. These are not merely criminal violations at a human level; they are insults against God as well. The problem is, there will always be vast numbers of people who do not see other people as sacred. And even if they do, there are no bounds to the avarice, cruelty, or malice out of which some people violate others.

In his seminal book, *The Locust Effect: Why the End of Poverty Requires the End of Violence* (Oxford University Press, 2014), Gary Haugen, director of International Justice Mission, documents how unrelenting cycles of crime against people and property, including modern-day slavery, are keeping vast numbers of people in the world today in extreme poverty. The only wide-ranging solution is to take away the incentive some people have to violate the dignity of others, and to have some reasonable form of criminal justice. "The poor don't have much in the way of money or possessions to steal—so it turns out that the most profitable thing to steal is the whole person."[4]

There is hardly a starker example of a violation of everything worthwhile than the tactic the Islamic State of Iraq and Syria (ISIS) has been using of beheading people and putting video of it online for the world to see. *New York Times* columnist David Brooks raised the question: why beheading? He writes:

The revulsion aroused by beheading is mostly a moral revulsion. A beheading feels like a defilement. It's not just an injury or a crime. *It is an indignity.* A beheading is more like rape, castration or cannibalism. It is a defacement of something sacred that should be inviolable. But what is this sacred thing that is being violated? Well, the human body is sacred. Most of us understand, even if we don't think about it, or have a vocabulary to talk about it these days, that the human body is not just a piece of meat or a bunch of neurons and cells. The human body has a different moral status than a cow's body or a piece of broccoli. We're repulsed by a beheading because the body has a spiritual essence. The human head and body don't just live and pass along genes. They paint, make ethical judgments, savor the beauty of a sunset and experience the transcendent. The body is material but surpasses the material. (italics added)[5]

I interviewed three women working with victims of human trafficking in Kenya. Nancy, Marcy, and Likoko run a church-based outreach for young women. Their experiences were the same as April's who has a similar ministry in Managua, Nicaragua. They all describe the psychological and spiritual bondage that is the consequence of the physical coercion of young women under the domination of men who hold them in bondage. Physical and sexual abuse go hand in hand with psychological abuse.

Indignity is a weapon in the hands of pimps who control the minds of the women they use. It is not just that they keep the women financially dependent, but they give the prostitutes they control a meager portion of the profits. They know exactly how to shape a woman's thought processes such that she is grateful for any small gift or favor she receives. She goes from *not being able* to leave, to not *wanting* to leave. The pimp brainwashes her into thinking that the only worth she has is what is bestowed on her by the pimp. She doesn't leave because she believes she would have no worth whatsoever on the outside.

There is only one way to reduce another person to that level of emotional dependence: take away all dignity, and then give back a sick, perverted sense of worth. If the woman does have a moment of clarity and leaves the pimp, chances are great that she will be back before long. This domination through indignity is so strong that even the small number of women who find their way into a recovery program with loving, accepting workers are continually at risk of abandoning their own rescue to go back to their slavery.

Virtually every society in the world today is riddled with patterns of abuse. What we need to understand is how pervasive abuse is because of its *usefulness* as a tactic of domination and control. Abusers gain something in the transaction. Abuse is not simply cruelty. Nonetheless, the personal dignity of victims even at this level of depravity can be restored.

## The Indignity of Illness

People lose their sense of worth not just when other people seek to reduce them, but when, in the natural course of life, they become physically afflicted. Illness diminishes us. It may lessen our sense of worth because we feel less capable. We may have a sense of uselessness. There is a sense of a loss of dignity, even though our worth is unalterable because it is determined by God.

This is certainly a challenge. When someone has to take leave of the work they do, they may lose a sense of purpose. When we are ill or disabled and become dependent on other people, we may have a strong sense of guilt about imposing on other people.

People who develop chronic illnesses or disabilities may live with the ever-present thought *I'm not the person I used to be*. This is more than *I'm not as strong as I used to be*. It gets to personhood. In the face of a serious or chronic condition, it is likely we will have angst about personal worth and even identity.

Our answer to the question "Who are you?" reveals our sense of identity. We may answer it from the perspective of origin: "I grew up in rural Texas." Or ethnicity: "I'm Asian American." Or gender, or generation, or social class, or religion. People with serious and chronic illness or disability may develop a core sense of identity centered there: "I am a diabetic." "I am a paraplegic." "I am a victim of ALS." It is unfortunate but understandable when people define themselves for life based on a characteristic that is not at the core of their being. But we must show respect by treating seriously ill people as more than their afflictions.

This is why we no longer call someone suffering from Hansen's disease a *leper*. Nor do we use diminishing and demeaning terms like *cripple*, *retarded*, or *crazy*. Likewise, *deaf and dumb*, *insane*, and *handicapped* are all terms best left in the past. Why? Not because of political correctness, but because of dignity. People with great physical challenges deserve the respect any person gets as created in the image of God. No person should be reduced to a label of diminishment.

In the image-saturated world in which we live, a world where "image is everything," the cheap and easy way to have relationships is to categorize people by crude social definitions. But everyone loses when even one person forgets his or her true identity.

A clearheaded concept of God-given dignity is our best defense against a diminished identity. This is the challenge: to accept that our bodies and minds may be weakened by disease, injury, or congenital conditions, but this doesn't take away our worth in the eyes of God.

## The Indignity of Aging

I was surprised that when I started getting some grey in my hair, it produced different reactions in people. Some family members found it a little unsettling. Friends I hadn't seen for years couldn't resist teasing me about it. I felt like I'd entered a new category with my professional peers: respected a bit more by some, but of less interest to others.

But when I travel overseas to Asia, Africa, or Latin America, the grey is no detriment—it is a benefit. Whether I am teaching or consulting or networking, I know that one begins with a baseline of credibility if you have been around the sun more times than your audience has.

In American culture today, there is a bias toward youthfulness. Television networks make sure we see people who have few wrinkles sitting in the anchor chairs. Bloggers who have barely begun their adult lives garner huge followings and are granted uncritical credibility based largely on how many subscribers they have. Communities that have an expanding proportion of senior citizens are viewed as declining. [6]

People who cross the 80-year mark soon find out that although they may still have the love of those they are close to, they feel less respected. Their opinions do not matter as much to some. Many people assume that older people's perceptions of today's world are skewed by their age, or that they want to live in the past (which makes no sense and is a logical impossibility anyway). Some assume they are out of touch. But what does that mean, really? Does lack of knowledge about the latest iterations of social networking apps mean these people lack knowledge about life? Who, after all is more expert about "tomorrow" if not those who have watched more "todays" turn into "tomorrows"? Someone who is 60 has moved from "today" into "tomorrow" 21,900 times. A 30-year-old, merely 10,950 times.

The social dynamics of all societies in the world are going to be tested in years to come, as the proportion of older people increases. According to the World Health Organization, by the year 2050 there will be 2 billion people in the world over the age of 60, compared to 605 million in the year 2000. The proportion of seniors, on a global scale, will double from 11 percent to 22 percent.[7] Communities will place themselves in a vulnerable spot if they do not consider older people as productive members and figure out ways to make that a practical reality. There is a price to a loss of worth.

When we view older people as having less worth and put them on the shelf, we not only violate their dignity, but we push ever-increasing numbers of people into dependency. This will result in ever-increasing economic stress. Lawmakers will be tempted to support "death with dignity" legislation (i.e., physician-assisted suicide) for the worst possible reason: not being able to afford as many old people anymore.

In the six months between my university days and starting graduate school, I took a job as a nursing assistant in a local nursing home. I worked in the quiet hours (third shift, from 11 p.m. to 7 a.m.) in the wing of the facility beyond locked doors. This section was for residents with severe enough dementia that they needed to be protected. The work was simple. Do rounds three times through the night with another nursing assistant, taking care of the physical needs of the residents (most of whom were incontinent) responding when someone was restless, and protecting when someone was in danger of falling out of bed. I learned all of their names, yet I wasn't able to have a single intelligible conversation with any of them.

I got to know them in the condition their Alzheimer's or other disease had left them, but I learned from family members what their personalities were like before the dementia diminished them. Walter was extremely combative, and was known to have a lightning-fast right hook if you were trying to help him with his sweater. Yet in his earlier life, he was a distinguished gentleman with a sweet spirit. So it was with the others.

I was conflicted about whether to think of these men and women as I saw them today, or as who they were before. But ultimately, I decided it did not matter. No human being can lose his or her dignity, in whatever state he or she is in.

One night the head nurse asked if I would sit with a lady whose vital signs showed she would not make it through the night. Her family lived far away. The nurse told me she shouldn't have to die alone, and that she wanted me to sit with her. I was 21 years old and hadn't watched someone die before. Throughout those hours in her darkened room the night was quiet. Her uneven breathing was the only noise I could hear, and the only thing I could think about. And when she exhaled that one last time, long and slow, I sat still for a while. What kept coming to mind was not the end, but the beginning: "Then the LORD God formed a man from the dust of the ground and breathed into his nostrils the breath of life, and the man became a living being" (Gen. 2:7).

Aging and illness challenge us to believe in worth even when our strength is ebbing. The durability of any society or culture is not measured by how it treats the strong and privileged, but whether it treats its weakest members with dignity.

## Indignity and Bureaucracy

One area of life where our worth or dignity can be most active is in our work, whether in an office or a home or a factory or a store or a coffee shop. Yet the way we work and the way we direct others in their work can also diminish people.

Made in the image of a creative and productive God, a God of labor and work, human beings are consummate builders. But there are upsides and downsides to building great things. Building with a motive of self-aggrandizement gets you a tower at a place called Babel, but it results in division and conflict. Creating a god you can see and touch, a god that glistens in the sun like the golden calf, will impress people at the same time that it diminishes them.

Robert Oppenheimer rued the day he helped create a fission bomb. The post–World War II hero Dwight D. Eisenhower denounced the "military industrial complex" that world war helped create. Today there are serious discussions about how automation and robotics could actually result in something that would turn on its creator someday.

One human invention that seemed to have the benefits of order and efficiency has time and again turned into systems that take something away from our humanity: bureaucracy. We all live in the midst of bureaucracies. Some bureaucracies work well. But most tend to get more and more complex and become systems which serve themselves. That is why we have bad experiences with them.

*Harvard Business Review* ran an article in November 2014, titled "Bureaucracy Must Die" by Gary Hamel. In it, Hamel analyzes the essential intent—and the weakness—of bureaucracy.

> What's the ideology of bureaucrats? Controlism. Open any thesaurus and you'll find that the primary synonym for the word "manage," when used as verb, is "control." "To manage" is "to control."

> Managers worship at the altar of conformance. That's their calling—to ensure conformance to product specifications, work rules, deadlines, budgets, quality standards, and corporate policies. More than 60 years ago, Max Weber declared bureaucracy to be "the most rational known means of carrying out imperative control over human beings." He was right. Bureaucracy is the technology of control.

But what are the implications of this "worship at the altar of conformance"? What happens when we treat people as cogs in a machine, as simply the means to an end?[8]

Unfortunately, managers often see control and freedom as mutually exclusive. But as long as control is exalted at the expense of freedom, our organizations will be less efficient than they might be in terms of human values. That is why Gary Hamel said bureaucracy must die. Think of what is gained when managers draw out of workers their native capacities for rationality, creativity, morality, and even spirituality. There is the moral question as well. The inherent dignity of workers, made in the image of God, requires respect. Work should be an extension of our humanity; it should not make us less than human.

It is not easy to invent new ways of working that will add value to workers and not take it away. But when it is accomplished, it is a wonder to behold. The alternative is unthinkable: that we will continue to create impersonal organizations that turn people into parts of machines. Disrespect of workers leads to disrespect by workers. And our work culture shapes the whole broader culture.

In this chapter we have looked at just a few ways in which human depravity attacks human dignity: the indignities of abuse, of illness, of aging, and of bureaucracy. There is so much more. Crime.[9] Racism.[10] Inequities in criminal justice systems.[11] Extreme poverty.[12] Religious persecution.[13]

All these social ills and spiritual corruptions have this in common: they diminish people. They either deny, insult, or corrupt human dignity. In some cases the denial of dignity is a tactic of control; in others it is the consequent damage that happens in a diseased and catastrophe-prone world.

To believe that dignity can be assailed but not lost is an article of faith. But there is more than that. Dignity *can* be restored, and it is, every day.

I sat one day on the stone steps along the Bagmati River in Kathmandu, Nepal where, on the other side of the river, there were seven or eight stone platforms. On each one was piled a stacks of logs on which lay the burning bodies of people being cremated. On some platforms there were stacks of logs, carefully placed, awaiting bodies. Some platforms contained nothing more than smoldering ashes. Along the stone pavement that lined the river, family members were attending to the bodies of their loved ones, pouring water over the bodies which were wrapped in bright orange shrouds. The rituals go on for hours. The crackling of the fires, the haze of the smoke, and the smell of the burning was very different from the rituals we observe in funeral homes back in the U.S. There is something telling about what we do with human bodies after death sets in.

One time in Kenya I was teaching a seminar on grief and mourning to a group of counselors, and the conversation suddenly took a lively turn as participants began describing, in detail, the burial rituals they follow in their different tribal groups. The rituals varied a great deal—some in homes, others outside, different durations of mourning and practices of burial. But they all had this in common: rites of burial all seek to dignify the person who has passed. A corpse is a lifeless object, but human beings speak loudly about their values when they recognize the summation of an earthly life with some solemnity and dignity.

In *Dignity: Its History and Meaning*, Michael Rosen acknowledges a kind of mystery in this: "the universally held belief that we have a duty to treat dead bodies with respect represents a deep puzzle for moral philosophy." [14] He also strongly believes that dead fetuses resulting from abortions need to be treated with dignity. [15]

I'm ending this chapter with these observations about burial customs, to point out that, in our rites of passage for those who have died, most people in most cultures believe it is right to assert dignity, and this is significant.

A fallen Marine may get a military funeral with full military honors, a Hindu may be ritually bathed by a surviving relative, a stillborn child may be honored with solemn prayers. The human instinct to do more with a body than just discard it is evidence that when we are slapped in the face by the indignity of death, we want to rise up and assert that the person who has passed is worth something. Dignity is not "a useless concept."

The question, of course, is what can be done while we are still alive to assert, defend, and restore dignity when mighty forces are working toward indignity. That is the subject of the next chapter.

---

[1] Laura Hillenbrand, *Unbroken: A Word War II Story of Survival, Resilience, and Redemption* (New York: Random House, 2010), 180-181.

[2] C. S. Lewis, *Out of the Silent Planet* (New York: Scribners, 2003), 129.

3 John Kilner, "The Impact of Sin on God's Image," in *Dignity and Destiny: Humanity in the Image of God.*

4 "There are more slaves in the world today (best estimate—27 million) than were extracted from Africa during 400 years of the transatlantic slave trade." Gary Haugen and Victor Boutros, *The Locust Effect: Why the End of Poverty Requires the End of Violence* (Oxford: Oxford University Press, 2014), 18.

5    David Brooks, "The Body and the Spirit," *The New York Times*, September 4, 2014.

6 *Ageism* is the term used in the last few decades for stereotyping and discrimination against people because of their age. According to the American Psychological Association, 80 percent of people over 60 report some kind of devaluing or discrimination against them. It may come in the form of poking fun at older people, but ageism is more serious when the mental health system ignores treatable conditions. Negative stereotypes may even shorten lifespan. ("Fighting Ageism," The American Psychological Association, May 2003).

7 According to the website of the World Health Organization, www.who.int/ageing.

8 Immanuel Kant, the philosopher who is most associated with the ideal of human dignity, believed the central truth of dignity is that people cannot treat each other as a means to and end. In the *Groundwork of the Metaphysics of Morals* (1785) he expressed it like this: "Act so that you treat humanity, whether in your own person or in that of another, always as an end and never as a means only." This conviction is what lies behind Kant's idea of moral duty as the basis for practical moral and legal decisions.

9  Nicholas Turner and John Wetzel, "Treating Prisoners with Dignity Can Reduce Crime," *National Journal*, September 15, 2015.

10  Mark Galli, "Hope in the Face of Intractable Racism," *Christianity Today*, July 22, 2015.

11  Gary Haugen and Victor Boutros, *The Locust Effect: Why the End of Poverty Requires the End of Violence*.

12  Jonathan Glennie, "The Saddest Thing in the World Is not Poverty; It's Loss of Dignity," *The Guardian*, January 28, 2015.

13  Paul Marshall, "Religious Liberty, the Center of Human Dignity," *Religion and Liberty* 10 (2000). Charles Chaput, "Of Human Dignity: The Declaration of Religious Liberty at 50," *First Things*, March 18, 2015.

14  Rosen, *Dignity: Its History and Meaning*, 129.

15  "May [a dead fetus] be treated any old how? Thrown in a rubbish bin? Flushed down a toilet? My conviction is that it too must be treated with dignity. But why?" Rosen (*Dignity: Its History and Meaning*, 134-135).

## Chapter 3

---

# Restoring Dignity

---

*True dignity abides with him alone*

*Who, in the silent hour of inward thought,*

*Can still suspect, and still revere himself,*

*In lowliness of heart.*

—William Wordsworth

Dr. Stephen Foster is 65 years old and runs a rural hospital in the West African country of Angola. For almost four decades, he has worked with meager supplies and staff in order to help anyone coming for medical care. One time he faced off with soldiers looking to kidnap his male nurses, standing his ground as the soldiers fired their AK-47s at his feet. He and his family live in constant risk, and they have done so for years. One of his sons contracted polio, a daughter had a life-threatening case of cerebral malaria, and their family was in danger of starving when war enveloped their region.

Dr. Foster gives medical treatment to women suffering with obstetric fistulas, a deforming consequence of poor conditions during childbirth resulting in continual incontinence of urine and feces. This horrific medical condition leaves many women in impoverished countries as social outcasts for life, rejected by their husbands, shunned by friends and family. Women cured by someone like Dr. Foster experience more than physical healing; they experience a restoration of dignity.

Dr. Foster lives in Angola because of his faith and a compelling sense of mission. There are many other heroes like Dr. Foster whose names hardly anyone will ever know.

These details come from a *New York Times* column [1] by Nicholas Kristof, who says: "I'm not particularly religious myself, but I stand in awe of those I've seen risking their lives in this way—and it sickens me to see that faith mocked at New York cocktail parties." [2]

Even in the greatest humanitarian work, no one is "giving" dignity to someone else. If we can give dignity, we can take it away. If dignity were merely social status, then it certainly can be given or taken away. But virtually all missions of mercy in the Christian tradition understand that helping people in their living conditions—health, education, freedom, justice—and thus with their status, is a consequence of a higher reality: all people created in the image of God possess inherent dignity or worth, and they are worth being helped when in distressing conditions.

What we can do, and must do, is *recognize* people's dignity in the eyes of God, to *reinforce* it, and to help people suffering indignities with a *restoration* of a sense of dignity and then live that out.

There are assaults on human dignity in every corner of the world today. We tend to think of places of political oppression, poverty, disease, widespread personal crime, lack of justice. But in developed countries, there is a crisis of dignity as well wherever people fail to recognize and respect the lives of the elderly, the indigent, the unborn, the mentally ill, and many others who are viewed as diminished in some way. Dignity and indignity are movements within whole societies, but their foundations are in the lives of individual people. Dignity is violated or restored one person at a time.

## Conformed to the Image of God's Son

One valid way of describing the gospel of Jesus Christ is that it is the promise of the restoration of dignity. God created humanity according to his image and his likeness, and thus invested humanity with incalculable worth. Because the human race has become twisted and corrupted by sin, barely reflecting Godlikeness, God chose to make redemption and restoration possible. This saving mission has many descriptions: reconciliation, justification, adoption, redemption, sanctification, glorification. The mission of Jesus was to seek and to save the lost. Father, Son, and Holy Spirit combine in this great saving feat, and human beings gain worthwhileness in the process. This is the gospel.

One of the most quoted verses of the New Testament is Romans 8:28: "We know that in all things God works for the good of those who love him, who have been called according to his purpose." It is the "all things" idea that catches our interest.

Almost everybody is trying to understand the mystery that life sometimes seems so good, and at other times so bad. "All things" are full of contradictions. The people we love the most are those who can hurt us the most. The natural world can be breathtakingly beautiful, and then turn into a hostile environment. You can go to Washington, D.C. and walk among the stately pillars and facades, the monuments to the fallen soldiers, the memorials to great leaders—and wonder how the government can be replete with so many weaknesses and engender such a low level of confidence in the populace.

Life is full of crosscurrents and contradictions. In almost every area of life we are left wondering: *Is there some good that can emerge from all these contradictions? What can be salvaged from "all things"?* So when Romans 8:28 says that "in all things" God works for the good of those who love him, we want to know how that works.

Just before Romans 8, the apostle Paul describes the inner spiritual battle within the self: "For I do not do the good I want to do, but the evil I do not want to do—this I keep on doing" (7:19). No wonder life is full of conflict and contradictions. No wonder we want to believe that somehow, "in all things God works for the good."

The very next sentence in Romans 8 describes how "all things" can somehow work out in the grand scheme of life. Here we find again the idea of humanity created in the image of God: "For those God foreknew he also predestined to be *conformed to the image of his Son*, that he might be the firstborn among many brothers and sisters" (8:29, italics added).

Here is the big picture. God created a world and a special class of creatures known as human beings as a spectacular expression of God's own glory, power, majesty, holiness, beauty, and love. But humanity became corrupted. Bent toward transgression; misguided by sin; blind to reality. Diminished, shattered, subject to every form of indignity. Men and women, gangs and governments, dictators and wife beaters and slave owners became the despoilers of dignity. And sometimes they construct whole bureaucracies of indignity or campaigns of murder.

God was not content to leave a broken world broken, and so a way of restoration was forged. This plan was "predestined," which means to be arranged ahead of time.

Paul's point here is that the proclamation about Jesus' mission and message was not a random innovation. No one spontaneously fabricated Jesus from Nazareth as savior figure.

The purpose of Jesus' mission was to make a way for the restoration of human nature for anyone ("to be conformed to the image of his Son"). The "image of [God's] Son" is not different from the creation principle of being created "in the image of God." Humanity was created in the image of God; Jesus is the perfection of humanity, and thus the perfect picture of what this image is (see Romans 5 and 1 Corinthians 15).

This is the dignity of Jesus—a worth or value that exceeds simple human value. He suffered indignities at the hand of human authorities, but his true worth was never compromised.

Art restoration is the attempt to return a work of art to its original or near-original appearance. The task of art restoration is difficult and controversial. Today's art experts look back on the attempts in past generations to restore sculptures and paintings—including using hydrochloric acid to clean up Michelangelo's *David*—as arbitrary preferences that may not restore the original form and ignore historical development.

But there is perhaps no greater disaster in art restoration than the job 80-year-old Cecilia Giménez did on a 1930 painting of Jesus on a pillar in a church in Broja, Spain, in 2012. Meaning well, this amateur ended up imposing on the painting her own brushstrokes, ending up with a Jesus who looked like a pale-faced ape ringed in fuzzy hair and a half-beard with a crooked mouth and hollow eyes. It would have been taken for vandalism, if it were not known that the woman really thought she was improving the representation of Jesus.

Even the highly professional and meticulous restoration of the Sistine Chapel in Rome, painstakingly carried out by restoration experts, is controversial. It seems to make sense that layers of grease and soot resulting from centuries of burning candles, when removed, would reveal the original image Michelangelo created. But the restoration process, in some experts' opinions, has compromised areas of light and shadow in the frescos. Nevertheless, the restoration results are stunning. Thousands of visitors now get a better idea of why this unique place had such value when it was created. It may not be perfect, but we have a better view of what Michelangelo intended when he painted the image of Adam, and the image of Creator God, the image of Christ coming in judgment, and so much more.

What does it mean for men and women to be restored to the image of God or, in the words of Romans 8:29, "to be conformed to the image"? The Greek word "conform" is *summorphos* from *sum*, "together," and *morphe*, "form." So we speak of trans-form-ation as essential change, form-ation as the incremental shaping of mind and personality, and con-form-ity as choosing to let one's character imitate the contours of the character or values of someone else whether it's a parent, a teacher, a celebrity, or some other exemplar.

Throughout the New Testament we find expressions of the "form" a human life can take. In an age where "image is everything," whole currents of our culture focus on "form" in a physical or material sense. Billions of dollars are spent on body-building, weight-losing, skin-preserving, tummy-tucking, chin-shaping, face-lifting. But what about the shaping of the soul?

Dignity is not restored by weight loss and body-building. It is a lifelong process of people choosing to live within the transforming power of the kingdom of God, of being "conformed to the image."

There is no problem in the human race that would not be remedied if men and women were conformed to the image of God and the image of God's Son. Vice is twisted back into virtue. Greed returns to desire. Lust is restored to longing. Malice melts. Envy evaporates. Anger as violence is tamed to anger as indignation. And pride as arrogance is reformed into that good and wholesome pride that is constructively ambitious.

That is just part of what being "conformed to the image" looks like on a personal level. But the greater work expands to social reformation. "There is neither Jew nor Gentile, neither slave nor free, nor is there male and female, for you are all one in Christ Jesus" (Galatians 3:28). In a single sentence the apostle Paul declared a reality that whole generations of attempts at social reform have tried to achieve. "There is neither Jew nor Gentile," means God's plan has blown past religious particularity. "Neither slave nor free" is a charter for economic reform. "Nor is there male and female" undermines millennia of gender discrimination and abuse.

For most of the history of Christianity, social reform has been seen as the natural consequence of personal reform. Integrity and consistency demand that the gospel that declares salvation for individuals be applied to all social relationships and social structures. On the other hand, a "social gospel" not grounded in personal transformation is futile. It is promising fruit without the tree.

None of this happens naturally. Being "conformed" to anything—even what promises to give purpose and fulfillment and dignity—has always cut against fallen human nature. We want what we want and we want it on our terms. That makes *conforming* a dirty word. Being "conformed to the image of God's Son" is also in direct violation of what some hold as the highest and perhaps only ultimate value: autonomy. For anyone who sees dignity as nothing more than autonomy, the idea of conforming is an insult.

Here is where Christians need to explain clearly that being conformed to the image of God's Son is not a losing proposition. And it certainly is not a loss of dignity. The restoration of Godlikeness, even if only incremental, is to regain our worth.

## Transformed into the Image of God's Son

The promise of spiritual transformation, and with it, the restoration of human dignity, is powerfully at work in the world. Writing to the believers in worldly Corinth, the apostle Paul described it this way:

> Now the Lord is the Spirit, and where the Spirit of the Lord is, there is freedom. And we all, who with unveiled faces contemplate the Lord's glory, are being *transformed into his image* with ever-increasing glory, which comes from the Lord, who is the Spirit (2 Cor. 3:17-18, italics added).

Romans 8:29 speaks of being "conformed to the image"; in 2 Corinthians 3 we find the idea of people "being transformed into [Christ's] image." This is a text not to be glossed over. First, this transforming work is accomplished by the Spirit of the Lord. It "comes from the Lord." We will never overcome our problems by sheer willpower and a plan to restore dignity. Only the power of God can overcome the dead-weight inertia of fallen human nature. Only the Spirit of God can make fallen human beings want something better than their own autonomy.

This restoration is a process. Paul does not say in 2 Corinthians 3:18 that "we have been transformed," but "we *are being* transformed" with "*ever-increasing*" glory. The gospel offers a definitive way to get on God's side, but the restoration of dignity is a longtime work.

Then Paul says that in this is "freedom." This is what so many find hard to believe, that in submission to Christ, there is real freedom. Martin Luther put it this way in his classic, *The Freedom of a Christian*: "A Christian is a perfectly free lord of all, subject to none. A Christian is a perfectly dutiful servant of all, subject to all." Many cannot accept the paradox that in servitude to God there is real freedom, the realization of all our true potentialities.

Christopher Hitchens, one of the most vocal evangelists for atheism in recent years, fatally misunderstood submission to God as a total loss of dignity:

> I don't want it to be the case, that there is a divine superintending celestial dictatorship from which I could never escape and that abolishes my private life. . . that would supervise me, keep me under surveillance in every moment of my living existence. And then, when I died, it would be like living in a heavenly North Korea where one's only

duty was to continue to abase oneself and to thank forever the Dear Leader for everything that we are and have. [3]

The tragedy of Hitchen's binary view is that either there is a God who is like Kim Jong-il, or there is no God at all. So we are left to choose between a very bad god, or to make ourselves sovereign. Neither option leaves us with real dignity.

We must not miss the significance of the "unveiled faces" in 2 Corinthians 3:18: "we all, who with unveiled faces contemplate the Lord's glory. . . ." This refers back to Exodus 34 which says that when Moses came down from Mount Sinai, "his face was radiant because he had spoken with the LORD" (Ex. 34:29). The phenomenon frightened the Israelites, so Moses put a veil over his face. It was not the only time in Scripture when something wondrous evoked fear.

But now, Paul says, everyone who is being transformed by the Spirit of God is a Moses. And it is time for the veils to come off.

This is authentic gospel witness. Not political machinations. Not naive social engineering. Not vitriol. Not religious tribalism. Not platitudes and spiritual cliches. The gospel is expressed in faces that reflect the glory of God, a glory that purifies and dignifies.

While walking along the dusty paths of a remote African village in southern Ethiopia, my missionary friend asked if I noticed differences in the faces of people we passed—the telltale signs of spiritual oppression in some, and of spiritual liberty in others. I certainly did. Some had a vacant look, narrowed eyes, drooping limbs, while others showed faces that were open and bright. You could see the effects of superstition and the fear of evil spirits and the curse of the witch doctor down the lane in the faces of some. And you could see real freedom, even a hint of glory, on the faces of those who had gained a faith in an all-powerful and endlessly gracious God.

Dignity is not just a philosophical proposition. It is at the core of human identity in theory and in lifestyle. Sometimes it is written on our faces. When we can work against all the indignities that life brings our way and come to the deepest conviction about the worth bestowed on us by God, we will be able to take authentic and humble satisfaction in life, and we will have the courage to defend and restore the dignity of others. This is the mandate of the gospel, the topic of the next chapter.

[1] Nicholas Kristof, "A Little Respect for Dr. Foster," *The New York Times*, March 28, 2015.

[2] Nicholas Kristof, "Evangelicals Without Blowhards," *The New York Times*, July 30, 2011.

[3] Christopher Hitchens, from an interview with Tim Russert, CNBC, June 30, 2007.

*Chapter 4*

---

# The Mandate of the Gospel

---

*Because men and women are made in the image of God, every
person, regardless of race, religion, color, culture, class, sex or
age, has an intrinsic dignity because of which he or she should
be respected and served, not exploited.*

—The Lausanne Covenant

We began with the question of the meaning of human
worth or dignity (chapter 1), which has historically been
answered from several angles. The biblical tradition an-
chors the worth of humanity in the creation—human
worth as a God-given innate reality that some ignore,
deny, or suppress, but cannot destroy.

Dignity as status is an alternative view which was true for Roman society in classical antiquity, and cultures with caste systems or rigid socioeconomic strata today. Status is a feature of any society in which class systems develop cultural biases where some people are seen to have value and others are not.

Then there is the view that dignity is about behavior. One's *worth* is determined by how *worthwhile* one's behavior is in social relationships. Leading a dignified life means being committed to worthwhile values, ethics, and manners. While all of us would like everyone in our lives to behave better, the question is whether good behavior produces dignity, or the other way around, that a clear sense of dignity can and must inspire better behavior.

The secular vision, stripped of anything remotely spiritual, religious, or metaphysical, limits dignity to autonomy. This can be a philosophical commitment (autonomy as the highest good) or a pragmatic preference (let me do whatever I wish to do).

One last view is that dignity itself is a worthless idea, an artifact of religion or of social bias, but not a useful concept today.

In chapter 2 we looked at some of the many faces of indignity, which is like a slap in the face. Indignity is real because depravity is real. Some indignities are foisted on one group by another, whether it be personal or institutional abuse. Other indignities like illness and aging come to us like unwelcome guests, but they do not necessarily cause a deep erosion of a sense of worth unless our culture reinforces that devaluation. And then there are systems of indignity like the cruder forms of bureaucracy, which use people as tools of productivity or value efficiency above humanity, treating men and women as if they were the gears of a machine. There are many other ways in which people experience indignity: crime, extreme poverty, broken criminal justice systems, religious persecution, abortion, and more. There are a thousand ways to devalue what is most valuable to God.

In chapter 3 we considered the restoration of dignity, first at a personal level, and then with social consequences. The "image of God" definition of humanity from Genesis shows up in the New Testament as the true identity of all men and women, the template upon which our lives must be conformed (Rom. 8:29) and the glory into which our lives may be transformed (2 Cor. 3:17-18).

## The Mandate of the Gospel and Human Dignity

So where do we go from here? If we are compelled to restore dignity, what should be our focus? How can we get beyond talking about dignity as a mere abstraction? If the restoration of dignity is part and parcel of the mandate of the gospel, where can proclamation be joined with action?

One of the most dignified acts we are capable of is recognizing and restoring the dignity of others. This is what Jesus did, at the very same time he tore down and promised future judgement for the depraved behavior of corrupted leaders. Jesus raised up people who were devalued by society—people with leprosy and blind people, women and Samaritans, children and tax collectors and common laborers. This is part and parcel of the *euangellion*, good news, gospel. In the synagogue in Nazareth, Jesus read from the scroll of Isaiah the prophecy that defined his mission:

"The Spirit of the Lord is on me, because he has anointed me to proclaim good news to the poor. He has sent me to proclaim freedom for the prisoners and recovery of sight for the blind, to set the oppressed free, to proclaim the year of the Lord's favor." (Luke 4:18-19)

The gospel says that, in Christ, God is restoring what is worthwhile by God's own estimation. Jesus' mission "to seek and to save the lost" (Luke 19:10) implies human worth and confers human worth. People are worth saving, by God's sovereign estimation. And human beings are invested with additive worth because of the restorative work of the Spirit of God. The gospel sets a mandate for people who count themselves followers of Jesus.

When I was in graduate school, I listened to a special speaker from Lebanon who was with us for one day. I remember his dignified demeanor and his sobering words, as he outlined ways in which civilization itself hung in the balance in the late 20th century. Few people can speak with credibility on such a soaring theme, but this was Dr. Charles Habib Malik, philosopher and diplomat, former Lebanese Ambassador to the United States and to the United Nations.

Dr. Malik (who held honorary doctorates from more universities than anyone else in the world) was the key intellectual leader in a small group of people who drafted the Universal Declaration of Human Rights in 1948 after the world had torn itself apart in two world wars. Dr. Malik was not only a diplomat, but a theologian respected by leaders in the Eastern Orthodox, Roman Catholic, Protestant, and Evangelical traditions. His influence is clearly seen in the declaration, especially in the insistence that inherent dignity is the basis for human rights. [1]

This document, forged at a time when leaders of the world wondered how humanity might survive the ravages of its own violence, begins with the words:

> Whereas recognition of the inherent dignity and of the equal and inalienable rights of all members of the human family is the foundation of freedom, justice and peace in the world. . . .

The document goes on to detail the rights of all people in matters of speech, religion, movement, thought, conscience, and more. Ambassador Malik was insistent that freedom of conscience, religion, and expression be integral to the statement.

The Universal Declaration is the most translated document in the world. [2] At its inception all the nations in the General Assembly voted for the declaration, except for abstentions from South Africa (which wanted to preserve apartheid), Saudi Arabia (which could not agree to the proposition that people should be free to change their religions), and the Soviet Union and Soviet block countries (which would not have been in favor of the right of movement; i.e., for people to leave their countries).

Human dignity is a social and philosophical value that can be held regardless of religious convictions. Dignity is an ideal embraced by believers and most secularists alike, though it may rightly be asked what the basis is for human dignity if there is no transcendent source for the value. Assigning worth would seem to require an external moral authority, typically understood to be God.

Anyone in any of the Christian traditions will see in the assertion of "inherent dignity" the historic rationale for human worth rooted in the creation principle of Genesis 1. Dignity is inherent because it is innate.

Why is this a time for dignity? There is no era in which it has been unimportant, but today we have so many new ways to erode and compromise any sense of dignity. Some voices are inviting us to give up on the search for dignity. The "worth" of one group contradicts the "worth" of another group, so, the argument goes, we are better off not looking above for any ideal about value.

So we stand at a crossroads with multiple alternatives. Will we continue to hold to the ideal of dignity? And if so, with what understanding? For Christians, dignity, with the gospel, is a call to action in this pivotal time in which we live. The call is expansive and universal, both inspiring and foreboding.

What follows are eight ways in which believers can follow the mandate of the gospel that also promote and restore dignity today. (There are, undoubtedly, many more applications, which ought to be the subject of further discussions.)

## 1. We must be examples of dignified living.

When Christians say they stand for human dignity but behave in disrespectful and undignified ways, they not only undermine their own message, but they sully the gospel. This is a scandal.

John Stott, the longtime rector of All Souls, Langham Place in London, chaplain to the queen, and as influential as any Evangelical Protestant in the 20th century, gave his final public address in July of 2007.[3] For this he saved his last appeal. The statement was neither novel nor rhetorical. His message: "I want to share with you where my mind has come to rest as I approach the end of my pilgrimage on earth, and it is this—God wants his people to become like Christ. Christlikeness is the will of God for the people of God."

Stott quotes Romans 8:29 about God's people being predestined to be conformed to the image of God's Son. He calls 2 Corinthians 3:18 about unveiled faces "a magnificent vision." And he says 1 John 3:2, which speaks of becoming like Jesus at his return, points to future complete transformation. So this is the comprehensive act of God, past, present, and future.

But "like Jesus" in what ways, specifically? In this final public address, Stott says there are five ways: *incarnation*, *service*, *love*, *endurance*, and *mission*. The *incarnation* of Jesus was unique, but the attitude of the incarnation, the humility whereby Jesus took a lower place, is to be the mind-set of the ordinary believer (Phil. 2:5-8). That alone distinguishes Christians, when they fight against human nature and choose humility.

Then there is Christlikeness in *service*, which Jesus commanded at numerous points in his ministry, depicted in the flesh when Jesus washed his disciples' feet, saying "you should do as I have done for you" (John 13:15).

Then, we are called to be like Jesus in *love*, defined in Ephesians 5:2 "walk in the way of love, just as Christ loved us and gave himself up for us as a fragrant offering and sacrifice to God."

Patient *endurance* is another characteristic of the life of Jesus that the New Testament charges disciples to repeat. First Peter, for instance, explains the redemptive possibilities of enduring in the face of unjust suffering.

Finally, Stott says that we are to be like Christ in his *mission*. In his remarkable prayer for his followers recorded in John 17, Jesus said that he would be sending his followers out into the world, just as he had been sent into the world on a redemptive mission.

Stott concludes with this convicting proposition: the biggest barrier to the Christian mission is Christians themselves. When we behave in ways that are un-Christlike, we contradict and undermine the very message we bear. To put it positively: if Christians were Christlike, the world would be utterly different.

Those who consider dignity a function of behavior certainly have a point. We all would prefer to live in communities where people truly respected each other while holding on to their own convictions. We know that William

Wilberforce made a commitment to fight the slave trade in 19th century England. But we should remember that his second commitment, was "the reformation of manners," by which he meant Christian belief showing itself in reformed, dignified behavior. His concern was in response to the coarseness of the culture of England at the time. [4]

But a life with dignity cannot be founded simply on a desire to be more polite and civil. That will be short-lived. We will consistently behave with dignity only if we have a deep conviction about inherent worth—of ourselves, and of others.

If we do not behave with dignity and treat others with dignity, any proclamation of the gospel will be confusing at best, and invalidated at worst. If there is one sin that Jesus identified more than any other, it was religious hypocrisy.

## 2. We must show freedom to be a better value than autonomy.

So much of the tension about the idea of human dignity arises out of the fear that if we accept dignity, we will lose personal freedom. This is an understandable fear, as freedom is not only a cherished value, but it also lies at the heart of the historic understanding of humanity made "in the image of God."

But freedom is different from absolute autonomy. The philosophy of autonomy says that society should grant individuals complete discretion in their moral and ethical choices. This is medical ethicist Ruth Macklin claiming autonomy as the highest value in her article: "Dignity is a useless concept: It means no more than respect for persons or their autonomy."[5]

In fact, no one lives in complete autonomy, and no one actually wants to assert autonomy as an absolute value, which would make ordered societies impossible. Ordered societies draw lines everywhere; it is just a question of where the lines are drawn. Even if you would like the freedom to pick vegetables at will out of your neighbor's garden, you want laws preventing your neighbor from doing that to you. Popular opinion may favor abortion on demand, but virtually no one thinks a woman should be able to terminate her pregnancy one week before her due date because she changed her mind about becoming a mother. Some people would like the autonomy to tell their doctors to end their suffering with a lethal injection, but they do not want their relatives to have the autonomy to make that happen for their own convenience. It is, of course, in legal decisions where the concept of dignity as autonomy is most likely to appear.[6]

True freedom is never unbounded. True freedom is not at its core about eliminating restrictions, but it is about releasing our capabilities. Freedom *to*, not merely freedom *from*. A convict released from prison gets out from behind bars, but is only free when he or she figures out how to live a stable life. So the prospect of freedom for any of us is that we will be able to flourish as we discover and train our talents, most of which require boundaries, definition, and discipline. Freedom must have form.

Freedom is a better value than autonomy. In the name of freedom, we may be compelled to sacrifice and serve. To be free we must subject ourselves to purpose and calling. Freedom requires definition. This is true in every dimension of life. Even our biology requires boundaries. Cells that are unbounded lead to malignancy. We call it cancer.

There is a caveat here for Christian witness. The proclamation of the gospel of freedom in Christ must be explained today with clear articulation and winsomeness, not as a set of religious laws. This gospel of freedom truly is liberating, but a nonbelieving world will not accept the gospel if it is explained purely in terms of behavioral constrictions. The gospel is a message for human flourishing, not merely a judgment against human failure. The whole gospel contains both conviction of sin and release from sin's curse and grip. The apogee of the gospel is freedom.

The dignity of Jesus (the topic of the next chapter) is the incalculable worth of his grace and truth. Jesus proclaimed freedom *with form*. Liberation from our spiritual enemies, and liberation into "the way, the truth, and the life." The early Christian proclamation is summed up in the simple: *Jesus is Lord*. That is where we discover the superiority of freedom to autonomy. Many, of course, reject the notion of *Jesus is Lord* out of hand (and, for that matter, any lordship of anyone other than the self). But just as the gospel spread like wildfire in the Roman Empire where pluralism offered a cafeteria of religions and philosophical schools, so today many will accept the lordship of Christ, knowing that they are giving up autonomy for the far greater gift of freedom.

## 3. We must be champions of dignity for those whose dignity is being violated.

> This is what the LORD says: Do what is just and right. Rescue from the hand of the oppressor the one who has been robbed. Do no wrong or violence to the foreigner, the fatherless or the widow, and do not shed innocent blood in this place. (Jer. 22:3)

It comes as a shock to many when they hear that there are more slaves in the world today than at any other time in history. On a single day in Chennai, India, 512 of them were freed from a brick factory when representatives of International Justice Mission (IJM) and Indian government officials entered the facility. The slaves included 23 children and many who were too old and frail to work, but they were still being held at the factory. They were subjected to 18-hour workdays, given little food and water, were regularly beaten by the supervisors, and their promised wages withheld.

When the IJM staffer asked the throng that had gathered in a courtyard who wanted to come out, hundreds of hands shot up. They were transported to a camp by the truckload, where they received medical care, food, and water. And they were interviewed by officials who would build a legal case against the owner of the factory, who was already under arrest.

Days later IJM staff delivered the men, women, and children to train stations so they could return to their homes—most of them 1,000 miles away or more. Most countries have laws that identify the criminality of abusers, but the laws are not backed up with any credible criminal justice system. Today, 4 billion people in the world live outside the protection of the law. They live in places where any police or court functions are hopelessly corrupt and dysfunctional. They have no rule of law, and so there is nothing shielding them from violence.[7]

As was the case with Louis Zamperini in the Japanese POW camps, the slave owners in Chennai—and in thousands of other locations today—use people as the cogs in their money-making machinery, by taking away any conscious awareness of dignity their victims previously possessed. This is a pathology in the human race that is as ancient as the Egyptians who held Hebrews as slaves. Many people have been made to believe they are worth nothing, and they will settle for the pseudo-worth of serving human masters.

The tactic works for despots who mentally enslave whole populations, and for pimps who want their girls to be psychologically twisted to believe the pimp loves them. And it works in average middle-class homes when one spouse systematically tears down the dignity of the other, knowing that it is possible to get someone with whom you are close to serve your every need, head bowed in servitude.

If we hold to the gospel of Jesus Christ, we must become champions for those whose dignity is being violated. That may mean intervening to help a friend or family member who is being erased as a human being without even being aware of it. It may mean financially supporting the good work of organizations like IJM that are actually freeing bonded laborers and sex workers, and doing long-term work transforming justice systems that are hopelessly broken. It certainly means being alert to the stories of victims, of keeping an open mind and a compassionate heart, of praying regularly for those who may have been convinced they are not worthy to pray to God themselves.

## 4. We must promote an ethic of work and productivity that supports the dignity of individuals.

Arthur C. Brooks, president of the American Enterprise Institute, has been writing about happiness in recent years. He contends that there are four values correlated with a sense of personal contentment and dignity: faith, family, community, and meaningful work. The last one, meaningful work, is not about how much money someone earns or the status one attains.

> The happiness rewards from work are not from the money, but from the value created in our lives and in the lives of others—value that is acknowledged and rewarded. That is what we call earned success. President Franklin Roosevelt had it right: "Happiness lies not in the mere possession of money; it lies in the joy of achievement, in the thrill of creative effort." The secret to happiness is earned success through honest work. [8]

Brooks speaks about the "deep truth" that:

> [W]ork, not money, is the fundamental source of our dignity. Work is where we build character.

Work is where we create value with our lives and lift up our own souls. Work, properly understood, is the sacred practice of offering up our talents for the service of others. [9]

Catholic theology has long emphasized the connection between work and dignity. In his 1981 papal encyclical, *On Human Work (Laborem Exercens)*, John Paul II wrote that the Genesis account of creation shows "what the dignity of work consists of: It teaches that man ought to imitate God, his creator, in working, because man alone has the unique characteristic of likeness to God." But the dignity of work is constantly threatened in the modern world, for instance, when people are treated impersonally as a "work force," as mere instruments rather than the subjects of meaningful work. John Paul II speaks in the encyclical of the dignity of the agricultural worker, of the physically disabled, and of the underemployed.

One common theme among those who write about dignity and work is that meaningful labor, of any kind, is vastly superior to people being given what they need by the state. [10] Another theme is that work is not a punishment, but a privilege. Toil may not be pleasant, and Christian conscience dictates that we protect people against unjust labor practices; but work itself is an essential dynamic of human life, rooted in the Genesis principle where God told Adam and Eve to tend the garden.

Christians, in general, are woefully underdeveloped in their understanding of work. The tragedy and the risk of this is when we think that we are spiritually significant only after we leave our places of work. For instance, when we go to church on Sundays. This leaves the majority of our lives detached from spiritual meaning, which is one sure way to keep our work limited to mere toil. This compartmentalization of life also steals from us the sense of dignity we should be experiencing in the ordinary flow of our daily work.[11]

## 5. We must reform bureaucracies that dehumanize.

We are good at creating bureaucracies to control behavior, but we don't know what to do when we find ourselves trapped in the machinery of the control systems we ourselves create. Control is an addictive experience. Anyone can be tempted to believe his or her worth goes up when he or she controls other people, instead of doing the harder task of influencing people toward freedom with form.

In the U.S. in the 1980s, there was a political push to impose mandatory minimum sentences. This resulted in a dramatic swelling of the population of jails and prisons around the country in the decades that followed. The motive was to reduce crime, and by some measurements that happened. But locking up people for decades who are guilty of nonviolent offenses, cramming them into over-crowded institutions, disrupting family structures, and putting an enormous financial burden on society, has been the hidden human cost, and, in many cases, a waste of human potential. The U.S. has 5% of the world's population, but 25% of the world's prisoners. 2.3 million Americans are behind bars. 95% of them will be released one day, and 2/3 of them will re-offend.[12]

One reason over-incarceration happens is because American culture is biased toward the quick and easy fix. It is simple to say "Lock 'em up." That rhetoric will win you an election if you are a politician. In America we like disposable pens, disposable cameras, disposable flash-lights. Why not disposable people? Is it any wonder that the public so facilely supports a widespread and sometimes thoughtless "lock 'em up" policy? We don't want the inconvenience of actually solving deep problems or of treating psychological conditions. The cheap and easy answer of "lock 'em up" puts many redeemable people in trash bins where they come out more damaged than when they went in.

We need the criminal justice system, but we must monitor it because any "system" tends to drift toward preservation of the system itself, losing sight of the original purpose. This is the nature of any bureaucracy.

The challenge we face is that the simplest way for us to bring order is to create a bureaucracy. This is true of prison systems, the military, businesses, and of institutions that we assume are high-touch but can be as bureaucratic as any other organization: schools, hospitals, and even churches. Bureaucracy is the easy way because control is the default instinct. Organizational efficiency is often gained at the expense of human dignity.

We need to ask ourselves whether we value freedom as much as we think we do. Do we respect others when they come up with ideas better than our own, or do we want to control so that we get the credit? When we enlist volunteer help, are we seeing volunteers as our means to get our ends accomplished, or do we view their purposeful engagement as a worthwhile end in itself? Are we willing to continually adapt and improve the rules of our organizations, knowing that a continual accretion of regulations will suffocate human freedom and ignore human worth?

Would we rather build the temple or the Tower of Babel?

## 6. We must respect the elderly and support those who suffer from physical or mental illness, or must cope with disabilities.

This is where dignity is intensely personal. Leaving aside the rhetoric, the philosophy, the public policy issues, we must choose dignity in every personal interaction we have with someone who could feel diminished because of unwelcome physical or mental decline. The work of dignity takes place most powerfully in the one-on-one interactions in which our attitudes toward the ill, the elderly, and the disabled are revealed.

Compassion is essential, but respect is equally important.

Respect is a choice we make. It does not come naturally to us. The easy thing is to bluntly categorize other people. After all, we're busy, we have things to do, places to go, goals to achieve. We don't want other people to get in our way or make our lives complicated. The real test of dignity lived out is the next conversation we have, and the values we communicate in it.

The word *respect* literally means to take another look. "Re-spect"—to look again.[13] That has to be intentional. Given the coarseness of our culture, it is time to stop and take another look. We are not at our best with our first impressions, which is when our biases and preconceptions are strongest. It is when we take the time to carefully, thoughtfully, and fairly look at someone else in our second and third impressions, when we "look again," that we begin to show respect.

It is time for us to dignify this present moment by the reverence we show for God and the respect we show toward the next person we talk to, whether it is someone we like or not. This is the "wisdom from above" that is "pure; then peace-loving, considerate, submissive, full of mercy and good fruit, impartial and sincere" (James 3:17).

It is never too late for us to take another look. To say to God: *Give me a new vision of the people around me;*

*help me to see them as you see them; elevate me above my prejudices.*

It is the reason Jesus said the whole Law is summed up in one simple truth with two parts: "'Love the Lord your God... and, 'Love your neighbor as yourself'" (Luke 10:27). The first is reverence, the second is respect. Jesus said: "Do this, and you will live."

There is, of course, a social dimension to all this. Across the centuries Christians have known instinctually that caring for those who are ill and disabled is part and parcel of the gospel of Christ. It is not the right thing because it pragmatically helps people accept the message. Respect is right because it is right. Mercy is right because it is at the heart of the gospel. Treating people with dignity is right because God has already determined that they have worth—and this is unassailable. There would be no gospel if there had not been an incarnation of God, and there would not have been an incarnation unless God had mercy toward the broken human race.

John Wesley and his core followers were at the center of a national spiritual revival in the 18th century that shaped Britain and expanded to influence America and the rest of the world. Proclamation of the saving mission of God in Christ was the tip of the spear, but this movement also produced a mighty social reform. The Methodists founded hospitals, dispensaries, orphanages, schools, and more.

People were perplexed that John Wesley would go to the miners of Bristol, a class of people considered subhuman by many, and proclaim the gospel to open-air assemblies when churches were closed to them. But this was the foundation of the Methodist Revival.

Society may be preserved if a grassroots movement helps to restore the dignity of people at every level, including those living at the lowest social ranks. Many historians think the Methodist Revival is a main reason why 18th century England did not go through a bloody revolution as happened in France.

## 7. We must build our bioethics on the foundation of human dignity.

In his book *Life, Liberty and the Defense of Dignity: The Challenge of Bioethics*, Leon R. Kass, M.D., sounds an urgent note about the complications brought on by rapidly advancing medical technology:

Modern medicine. . . . is daily becoming ever more powerful in its battle against disease, decay and death, thanks especially to astonishing achievements in biomedical science and technology. . . . Yet contemplating present and projected advances in genetic and reproductive technologies, in neuroscience and psychopharmacology, in the development of artificial organs and computer-chip implants for human brains, and in research to retard aging, we now clearly recognize new uses for biotechnical power that soar beyond the traditional medical goals of healing disease and relieving suffering. Human nature itself lies on the operating table, ready for alteration, for eugenic and neuropsychic "enhancement," for wholesale redesign. In leading laboratories, academic and industrial, new creators are confidently amassing their powers and quietly honing their skills, while on the street their evangelists are zealously prophesying a posthuman future. For anyone who cares about preserving our humanity, the time has come to pay attention. [14]

Dr. Kass, who teaches at the University of Chicago, acknowledges that human dignity is a contested concept in medical circles, elusive and misunderstood. But he offers a dire warning unless we hold to the principle of dignity: the same technology which is doing wonders for health and longevity will increasingly be misused out of motives of profit, pleasure, and a desperate fear of death. The way we treat people medically can take more away from our humanity than it restores. Medical ethics has always been important; it becomes desperately important the more abilities to engineer the human body and psyche we develop. Aldous Huxley's novel *Brave New World* about a new world order in 2540 is upon us already.

Abortion looms large as an ethical choice that clearly is based on one's view of the nature of the unborn and whether the fetus has worth or dignity. The sanctity of unborn human life does not hinge on a single concept like personhood, which many people will never accept for a fetus in the first trimester, for instance. A more direct line of reasoning is to ask: Is a fetus human? And is it alive? If the answer is yes to both then we know the unborn is human life, and it follows that this human life deserves respect and protection.

Unfortunately, the legal battles over access to abortion have eclipsed the moral and ethical question. In recent decades we have talked mostly about legal rights, which has supplanted deep personal moral reflection. This is a tragedy.

Polls show that a majority of Americans think abortion is wrong, but a majority also believe that women should legally have the freedom to choose. There is also a kind of paralysis when it comes to the medical realities of abortion. Videotaped exposés of abortion clinic personnel showing a shocking callousness when talking about fetal body parts and even their marketability do not seem to move public opinion very far on abortion policy. Clement of Alexandria in the second century warned that resorting to abortion kills embryos and, "along with it, all human kindness." [15]

It is tragic that there is so little public discussion about the nature of the unborn, because we have so much focused on the legal question. This does not need to be. A broader understanding of human development in the womb will allow women to make informed choices (though some ideologues charge that medical education on this point amounts to propaganda). What will not work is the old paradigm of defining human life by trimester distinctions, which has always been contradicted by the unbroken continuity of the developmental process.[16]

We would do well to shift our discourse about abortion to the ethical.

And then there are end-of-life bioethical issues. The maxim "death with dignity" has been used for over half a century now to mean that the end of life should not have to be dehumanizing or filled with unrelenting suffering. There is little controversy that mechanisms like advance directives have given physicians better guidance on whether or not someone wants heroic measures to be taken if they develop a terminal condition. Christian ethics would say there is nothing immoral about letting the process of dying unfold naturally.

But "death with dignity" has become the slogan of groups promoting physician-assisted suicide (or, as they would say, "physician-assisted dying"). This is a classic case of equating dignity with autonomy. "Death with dignity" here means the individual legally getting medical assistance to die at the time of their choosing. The historic religious and ethical objection is that we cannot play God with the time of our death. The social objection thus far, at least, has been that there is no sure way to make certain that a person is not making that fateful decision out of a temporary state of despair. Four U.S. states allow physician-assisted suicide now. If more do in the future, it will be because more legislatures view autonomy as the ultimate human value.

We are facing enormous bioethical challenges today, and they will only increase as our knowledge and technical capabilities increase. As complex as these issues are, it is crucial that these decisions not be left solely to technicians, scientists, and politicians. Who will resist the pressure to clone human beings? Who will tell a couple that they cannot collect the DNA of their terminally ill child in order to make a duplicate later? Who will prevent the sale of organs to the highest bidder on the black market?

Our greatest vulnerability in bioethical decisions is when we view human beings as bodies, and not as living souls.

## 8. We must rise above all forms of prejudice.

How easy those words are to say, but so difficult to do. We benefit from our biases; we profit from our prejudices. Partiality, intolerance, and discrimination are cheap and easy ways to navigate life. We are wired to look for our own tribe, and to hold members of other tribes at arm's length (or point guns at them or put them in prison). But the apostle Paul really meant it when he said: "There is neither Jew nor Gentile, neither slave nor free, nor is there male and female, for you are all one in Christ Jesus" (Galatians 3:28). This really is good news. Human beings are not the same, but they deserve equal and impartial treatment. There is no dignity for anyone, if it is not for everyone.

These eight examples of the mandate of the gospel and dignity, as substantial as they are, are just the beginning of the diligence required in the world as we know it today. This *is* a time for dignity. A biblical view of human worth, and of our propensity to depravity, requires us to examine every area of life to see if we are valuing what God values. Life in the 21st century presents a dizzying array of moral choices, equally true for the farmer in rural Africa earning $300 per year, and a CEO of a company in Dallas. Sometimes the person who has little understands worth and happiness more than someone who has everything.

We should call the defense of dignity a part of the mandate of the gospel because the mission of Jesus, to seek and to save the lost, is a statement of the value that God places on the lives of women and men, boys and girls. The question is whether we will have the courage and the commitment to actively assert the values we get from God.

---

[1] Ambassador Mary Ann Glendon writes, "No individual played a greater role in shaping and securing consensus for the UN's 1948 Universal Declaration of Human Rights, and. . . none of the framers reflected in greater depth on the dilemmas of human rights. . . . Malik saw man as uniquely valuable in himself, but as constituted in part by and through his relationships with others—his family, his community, his nation, and his God." Mary Ann Glendon, *A World Made New: Eleanor Roosevelt and the Universal Declaration of Human Rights* (New York: Random House, 2002), 1, 3.

[2] The UDHR, as of 2010, has been translated into more than 300 languages, from Abkhaz to Zulu, according to the Office of the High Commissioner for Human Rights, www.ohchr.org.

[3] Links to get to the text or the audio recording may be found at the website of The Langham Partnership.

4 Wilberforce not only opposed slavery; he also worked to improve the culture of a people who relished the entertainment of public hangings, of public dissection of dead criminals, and of bloody animal spectacles including the practice of bull-baiting (bulls being torn apart by thick-jowled dogs in public squares). Corruption and immorality were widespread—a fourth of the women of London worked as prostitutes. The aristocratic class protected their privileges with no thought of equity or justice.

5 Cited in chapter 1, along with Steven Pinker's article, "The Stupidity of Dignity."

6 Explaining the 5-4 decision of the U.S. Supreme Court regarding gay marriage in *Obergefell v. Hodges*, Justice Anthony Kennedy used dignity as autonomy as one of the four main reasons for asserting a universal right to gay marriage. "Four principles and traditions demonstrate that the reasons marriage is fundamental under the Constitution apply with equal force to same-sex couples. The first premise of this Court's relevant precedents is that *the right to personal choice regarding marriage is inherent in the concept of individual autonomy*" (italics added). The decision uses the word *dignity* 30 times. There were several dissenting opinions by other justices, including Justice Thomas who asserted that dignity is not a quality conferred or removed by the government: "Slaves did not lose their dignity (any more than they lost their humanity) because the government allowed them to be enslaved. Those held in internment camps did not lose their dignity because the government confined them. And those denied governmental benefits certainly do not lose their dignity because the government denies them those benefits. The government cannot bestow dignity, and it cannot take it away."

7 "More than 500 Free from Slavery in IJM's Largest Operation Ever," website of International Justice Mission, June 24, 2011.

8 Arthur C. Brooks. *The Conservative Heart: How to Build a Fairer, Happier, and More Prosperous America* (New York: HarperCollins, 2015), 32.

9 Brooks, *The Conservative Heart*, 97. Brooks speaks as an economist, but also as a committed Catholic. So he speaks of "the sacred practice of offering up our talents for the service of others."

10 "All labor that uplifts humanity has dignity and importance and should be undertaken with painstaking excellence." Martin Luther King Jr. speech at NYC Local 1199 "Salute to Freedom" program, March 10, 1968.

11 There are far too few books like Tom Nelson's excellent *Work Matters: Connecting Sunday Worship to Monday Work* (Crossway, 2011).

12 Statistics from Prison Fellowship, www.prisonfellowship.org as of Sept. 2015.

13 Late Middle English: from Latin *respectus*, from the verb *respicere* "look back at, regard," from *re-* "back" + *specere* "look at."

14 Leon Kass, M.D., *Life Liberty and the Defense of Dignity: The Challenge for Bioethics* (San Francisco: Encounter Books, 2002), 4.

15 *Paedagogus*, 2.10.96.1

[16] Ethicist David Gushee says: "The flaw of any trimester scheme, really any naming scheme (conception = zygote//two weeks = embryo//nine weeks = fetus//live exit from birth canal = newborn), is its incapacity to fully account for the unbroken daily continuity of the developmental process. Each step builds on the one before, as each milestone precedes the next one." (David Gushee, *The Sacredness of Human Life*, 358).

*Chapter 5*

---

# The Dignity of Jesus

---

*Worthy is the Lamb, who was slain, to receive power and
wealth and wisdom and strength and honor and
glory and praise!*

—Revelation 5:11-12

In 1857, archaeologists excavating the Palatine Hill in
Rome came across a peculiar inscription carved in the
plaster of a wall. It depicts a cross, the Roman method of
torturous and humiliating execution, upon which is a hu-
manlike figure with the head of a donkey. Off to the side is
a young man, one hand raised in the air as an apparent

gesture of adoration. The caption reads: *Alexamenos sebete theon*. "Alexamenos worships (his) God."

The scholarly consensus is that this graffiti was anti-Christian mockery, not just of Christians and their devotion, but of the object of their devotion, Jesus himself. The graffiti was created sometime in the second century. The shocking conclusion then, is that this cynical picture of a donkey on a cross may be the earliest visual depiction we have both of Jesus and of the crucifixion of Jesus.

Either the crucified Jesus is a person whose work culminated in the greatest act of saving sacrifice the world has ever seen, or it is the pitiful failure of a naive self-appointed prophet who misled many. The crucified Jesus is, in other words, of inestimable worth or utterly worthless. Whatever citizen of Rome decided to crudely sketch a donkey on a cross had made up his mind.

## Jesus, the Image

More than a century before the image of a donkey on a cross was etched into a plaster wall, the apostle Paul taught that in Jesus of Nazareth we find the very image of God. The image of God in Jesus is greater than the created likeness spoken of in Genesis 1, for the Son of God was an agent of creation and is "before all [created] things."

> The Son is the image of the invisible God, the firstbor over all creation. For in him all things were created: things in heaven and on earth, visible and invisible, whether thrones or powers or rulers or authorities; all things have been created through him and for him. He is before all things, and in him all things hold together. (Col. 1:15-17)

Jesus the Christ possesses ultimate worth, and so we may speak of the dignity of Jesus. Being "over all creation," being the agent of the creation of all things in heaven and on earth—including every authority and every power, and being the force whereby "all things hold together," the Son of God is more worthy than any person or any institution. This is why the early Christians' instinct was to pray to Jesus and worship Jesus, just as believers submit to God.

The writer of the book of Hebrews uses language similar to "image" when Jesus is described in this way:

The Son is the radiance of God's glory and the exact representation of his being, sustaining all things by his powerful word. After he had provided purification for sins, he sat down at the right hand of the Majesty in heaven. So he became as much superior to the angels as the name he has inherited is superior to theirs. (Heb. 1:3-4)

The Gospel narratives also depict a Jesus of astonishing honor and worth. Jesus is the perfect picture of integrity because every part of his life was consistent with every other part. Jesus did not fabricate a public persona. He did not shape his image for political effect. Oftentimes he declined to explain his actions or to elucidate his teachings.

Jesus humbled himself, but he did not let anyone take advantage of him. He expended himself for the sake of the needy in the crowds that pressed in upon him, to the extent that he retreated sometimes, physically exhausted. He wept over his people. His heart was broken that the people were like sheep without a shepherd. He prophesied that the Jews would suffer the indignity of being further crushed by their Roman oppressors. He foretold a day when the symbol of the unique worth of the Jews, the temple, would be broken and burned. Less than 40 years later, the temple of Jerusalem was in fact destroyed by the Romans.

## Jesus Restores Dignity

Jesus restored the dignity of many. Just speaking to the woman at the well gave her honor. People with leprosy were not only healed, but gained readmission to the community. A blind man Jesus healed was able to stand before the authorities and testify to a new thing God was doing (John 9). Jesus dignified close friends with his presence, including women who would stand with him through the crucifixion and mourn at his tomb.

Jesus made very ordinary men his key representatives, showing the inherent worth of fishermen, a tax collector, a political rabble rouser, and others whose backgrounds are obscure to us. These were not men of outstanding personal virtue. Simon Peter, on the day Jesus called him to follow, went down on his knees, saying, "Go away from me, Lord; I am a sinful man!" (Luke 5:8). One of them, Judas, was capable of abject betrayal, showing that depravity is only one ill-conceived idea away.

In the decades following Jesus' death and resurrection, these ordinary men and women who followed Jesus imitated his life. They aspired to model their lives on his image, even to the point of being like Jesus in death.

## Jesus and Indignity

Life will always be a struggle between dignity and indignity. The writer of the book of Hebrews, in the well-known twelfth chapter, speaks about the "struggle against sin" (v. 4) and the opposition coming from ill-willed people (v. 3). These are perennial problems not remedied by sheer force of will. In verse 2 the writer says believers must fix their eyes on Jesus. "For the joy set before him he endured the cross, scorning its shame, and sat down at the right hand of the throne of God."

The purpose of crucifixion was to terrorize and to shame. In Jesus' case, the execution had these additional humiliating features: the trial, the subterfuge of the religious authorities, the flogging, the robe, the sign above his head, the mocking of a thief.

The crucifixion of Jesus was the harshest act of indignity in history.

Because of who Jesus was and is, the shame of the cross is absolute. On the day of Jesus' crucifixion, the one human life in all of history that should never have been punished, had no crime or flaw of character, was abused and discarded.

And that is why any person today who is injured or limited by any of the indignities of life, can know that "the pioneer and perfecter of faith" went ahead of them (Hebrews 12:2). Jesus is the Savior of all, including those not deemed worthwhile by anyone anywhere.

What does it mean that Jesus "scorned" the shame of the cross? And what was "the joy set before him"? Bishop Stephen Neill said: "the death of Christ is the central point of history; here all the roads of the past converge; hence all the roads of the future diverge." [1]  There are many words that describe what Jesus accomplished by enduring and scorning the shame of the cross: *redemption, reconciliation, justification, adoption,* etc. And it is this also: the grace-filled beginning of being restored to the image of God. The joy set before Jesus was his knowledge that forgiveness and divine power would allow human beings to begin to be restored to the dignified form in which they were created.

## Jesus Worthy

The first image of Jesus in the book of Revelation, chapter 1, establishes that Jesus is victor over evil. A robed figure with a golden sash around his chest, white hair, and eyes blazing like fire. His feet glow, his voice is like the sound of rushing waters, his face shines like the sun, and a sword emerges from his mouth, a symbol of the word of judgment (Revelation 1:13-15).

The next image of Jesus, in Revelation 5, shows him as the object of adoration and worship. All of creation proclaims Jesus *worthy*:

> Then I looked and heard the voice of many angels, numbering thousands upon thousands, and ten thousand times ten thousand. They encircled the throne and the living creatures and the elders. In a loud voice they were saying: "Worthy is the Lamb, who was slain, to receive power and wealth and wisdom and strength and honor and glory and praise!" (Revelation 5:11-12)

Jesus is *worthy*. This is the dignity of Jesus whereby he restores our dignity. Christians around the world and across the ages have worshipped God the Father, Son, and

Holy Spirit, week after week in a great cycle of worth-giving. Worship is the acknowledgment of worth (worth-ship), and it leads us to a conformity that liberates. So we should know this. This should not be controversial. Jesus' person and mission has charged us with the work of recognizing, affirming, defending, and restoring the dignity of anyone who has given up on his or her own dignity, or is having it stomped on.

To say "this is a time for dignity" would be nothing more than wishful thinking were it not for the fact that worth-giving restoration is the stated intention of God: Father, Son, and Holy Spirit, both now and forever. The question is, *will we enter into the restoration?*

---

[1] E. M. B. Green, ed. *The Truth of God Incarnate* (London: Hodder and Stoughton, 1977) p. 80.

How do you see the issues of dignity, crisis, and gospel today? Share your thoughts at. . . .

www.wordway.org/dignity